Cheltenham Racecourse

CHELTENHAM RACECOURSE

ALAN LEE

PELHAM BOOKS

First published in Great Britain by
Pelham Books Ltd
44 Bedford Square
London WC1B 3DP
1985
©1985 by Alan Lee

British Library Cataloguing in Publication Date

Lee, Alan, 1954–
    Cheltenham Racecourse.
    1. Cheltenham Racecourse (Cheltenham,
    Gloucestershire)—History
    I. Title
    798.4′006′842416   SF324.4.G7

    ISBN 0-7207-1572-5

Printed in Great Britain by Butler & Tanner Ltd,
Frome and London

For permission to reproduce copyright photographs the author and publishers are grateful to the following:

Associated Press page 38; BBC Hulton Picture Library page 41; Cheltenham Art Gallery page 9; *Cheltenham Chronicle* pages 22, 23, 24, 28, 30; Cheltenham Newspaper Co. page 43; Gerry Cranham frontispiece and pages 63, 80, 93, 99, 131, 132, 134, 136, 142, 145, 149, 155; Bernard Parkin pages 11, 14, 15, 17, 18, 20, 39, 46, 51, 53, 55, 59, 67, 69, 71, 75, 78, 81, 90, 91, 94, 104, 107, 109, 115, 121, 129; George Selwyn page 84; Sporting Pictures (UK) Ltd. page 73; *The Times* page 32

Chapter 1

HE WAS NOT VERY OLD, early twenties maybe. His denim-clad legs had slipped from under him and were now straddling the pavement while he leaned, half-sitting and half-lying, against a convenient brick wall. His head was in his hands, though whether in remorse for heavy losses or heavy drinking, it was impossible to say.

The gates of the racecourse were still in sight, no more than fifty yards away. If only he had trusted himself to look up he would have seen two sleek American limousines gracefully pull up together and a male passenger emerge from each to loudly discuss the next port of call. In one car, seated next to the chauffeur, a lady with too much mink and make-up was on the mobile phone, no doubt talking to a rich girlfriend in Kentucky.

They came from different worlds, the swank Yanks and the fallen footslogger. But for at least the length of this fast-fading day they had been united, if only like passing strangers on the guest-list of an unsuitable wedding. They may have shared a patch of the lovingly tended lawn, they may possibly have cheered home the same horses and celebrated in their own special ways, bubbly or beer. Now, as the long, luxurious cars swept noiselessly onto the roundabout, taking the town centre road and passing the prostrate form on the pavement, unnoticed and unidentified, the curtain had come down for another twelve months.

Cheltenham is certainly theatre. From the spectacular backdrop, which no set designer could match, to the vivid talent and personality of the equine and human stars, to the mountain of unseen and largely unappreciated backstage work – all the components are there. And just as any theatre company will feel flat when the last night of a run is over, being inside Cheltenham racecourse on Gold Cup night is like intruding on a Christmas family gathering when the presents have been opened and all the food and drink has been consumed. Faces slowly drop with realisation that the fun is over, the mundane will soon return. Everyone forces a smile which nobody genuinely feels as, briefly, they forget how much stress and strain was involved and yearn to turn back the clock.

It is a little different for the punters. The fellow flat out and nauseous may not, of course, have felt entirely convinced he had enjoyed himself but, given two aspirins and a lie-in, the day would take on an altogether rosier hue and he would happily recall the winning bets and the belly-laughs. As for the rich Americans, well, after a good dinner, more champagne and a few hours sleep in a vastly overpriced hotel bedroom they would be ready to relate all the simply wonderful stories of the occasion to their equally rich, envious friends back home. They were the guests at the party. They didn't have the cleaning-up to face in the morning.

Cheltenham does not have to get by on one thrash each year. Outside the three-day National Hunt Festival there are thirteen further days' racing in a season, none so rich or distinguished as that magical March week but all attractive to the followers of what is, despite its growing international flavour, a peculiarly British sport.

These supporting events draw crowds running into several thousands and provide varied, often spectacular entertainment. Yet they pass unnoticed by most of the country. There are even plenty of people living in Cheltenham itself, blissfully unaware that their local racecourse is ever used outside that week in early Spring when a special kind of madness descends on the Cotswolds' traditionally sleepy spa town.

It is a madness which attracts money by the millions and creates employment for thousands. It brings some dreams to reality, takes others to destruction. It makes heroes by the handful, mugs by the score, and gets people drunk on every concoction of alcohol and emotion. It shortens tempers, lowers bank balances and yet somehow lifts the spirits. It is getting bigger and madder by the year.

The March Festival of 1984 was played out before record crowds who paid a record amount of money to get in and gave a record amount to the bookies. They watched races worth a total of £410,000, a record for any three-day meeting in Britain, and some of them did their watching from a plush new grandstand extension which had cost a cool £2.5 million, no doubt some sort of record in itself.

Cheltenham has long since ceased to be a country racecourse which just happens to stage the odd major meeting. It is big business, run on efficient and profitable lines, as evidenced by the foresight of Racecourse Holdings Trust, who own the place. Their initial outlay was £240,000 for a company which had shown a profit of £30,000 on their most recent balance sheets.

This would all seem like so many telephone numbers to the folk of the early nineteenth century. Especially those who crowded onto the grassy banks of Cleeve Hill, high above the existing Prestbury Park course, in August of 1819 to witness the first running of the Cheltenham Gold Cup. It was not quite the same thing as we know today. For a start, it was worth just 100 guineas to the winner, who happened to be a Mr Brodenham and his horse Spectre. For another thing, the Gold Cup started life

8

The first Gold Cup was a flat race run in 1819 on Cleeve Hill, high above the present course at Prestbury Park.

as a three-mile race on the flat!

There would probably never have been a Gold Cup, indeed never been a racecourse at Cheltenham at all, but for the far-reaching decision of King George III to try out the newly discovered mineral spring waters on his poor health in the summer of 1788. This was the raising of the white flag – the cavalry charge was under orders and what had previously been an insignificant market village was about to be swamped by the country's ample quota of what would now rather rudely be called social climbers and health freaks. The town became a byword in all the best circles. You just had to have been there. And so the place bulged and amenities appeared, like the racecourse.

Perhaps old King George does not deserve all the credit, however, for the story goes that many years earlier, in 1716, when Cheltenham boasted little more than a pretty, well-stocked trout stream and a solitary church for its few hundred inhabitants, a badly injured horse drank the spa waters and was miraculously cured. It would be altogether more apt to imagine that word spread through the recovery of the animal rather than the whims of the monarch and that the world's greatest racecourse was created, at least indirectly, by a horse.

Whether that horse eventually lived a long and happy life is not recorded. But the field in which he drank so momentously has long since disappeared, covered now by the Cheltenham Ladies' College, and it was a full century after his recovery when racing was finally launched, slowly at first but then to such growing acclaim and enthusiasm that, inside ten years, a grandstand had been built and the course seemed bound to take its place among the most prominent in England. Indeed, some estimates put the crowd for the 1825 meeting on Cleeve Hill as high as 50,000, a figure to be envied even today.

Not everyone, however, looked upon the races with interest or indulgence. They don't now, of course – one has only to speak to a few dozen local residents during the Festival week to discover that some are as hostile to the meeting as they would be if a sewerage works had sprung up next to their home. In the mid-1820s, the racing opposition manifested itself more vocally, and ultimately more violently, due largely to the influence of a striking young man named Francis Close.

Upon his appointment as curate at Cheltenham's Holy Trinity Church, Close quickly gained himself a following for his powerful preaching and, according to some accounts of the time, appeared to be making it his life's ambition to rid the community of all forms of gambling. Racing, being so popular, was his principle target, and he soon discovered there was considerable sympathy for his views within the town. In 1827 he was 'promoted' and, as vicar of the parish church of St Mary's, he was now in the ideal position to wage his holy war. He did so with undiminished gusto and, in June, preached a sermon of great force and conviction, entitled: 'The evil consequences of attending the racecourse, exposed.'

His Christian antipathy to the pleasures of the turf was taken up in what seems an unchristian manner by his disciples, a large group of whom set about disrupting the 1829 race meeting by any means at their disposal, including the hurling of abuse and objects at the horses and their riders. That meeting was completed despite the demonstrating so, the following year, the churchgoers took action which would have done justice to the soccer hooligans of today. They burned down the stand.

Racing has traditionally encountered opposition from the church all over England. Lambourn, the downland Berkshire village dominated by stable-yards, once had a parish vicar whose sermons were every bit as hostile as those of Dean Close. But the locals there who agreed with him did not go so far as to commit an act of arson.

It was never indisputably proved that the fire was started deliberately. Some called it an act of God. Most were more cynical. The upshot, anyway, was that the Cleeve Hill course was temporarily abandoned and, in 1831, a new course was used for the first time, sited on Lord Ellenborough's acreage at Prestbury Park. Although, later that century, there was a gap of almost fifty years when the new owner of the park flatly refused to accommodate the sport on his land, the modern-day home of National Hunt racing had been launched ... as a flat-race course.

Flat racing died a quiet death in Cheltenham during the 1840s, due in no small way to the continued preachings of morals by Francis Close. Somehow, steeplechasing not only survived but positively prospered and in 1834, on a three-mile cross-country course from the nearby village of

Prestbury Court Stables. Here trained Tom Oliver, Adam Lindsay-Gordon and John Roberts (who trained the 1954 Gold Cup winner Four Ten).

Andoversford, a properly regulated chase was held in the county of Gloucestershire for the first time. It subsequently became known as the Grand Annual Steeplechase and, 150 years later, it was the sixth race on the opening day's card at the 1984 Festival.

Among the prominent riders in that first running of the Grand Annual was a man named Tom Oliver, perhaps the most colourful of all the racing characters who were now making their home in Cheltenham. Certainly, his background is the stuff of romantic novels, his life an unstoppable rollercoaster which took him from triumph to disaster and back again, many times over. Unquestionably, however, he was a major influence in perpetuating racing in Cheltenham and the elderly locals still relate stories of him which they, in turn, were told as boys.

Oliver's ancestors were apparently Spanish smugglers who landed on the south coast of England and settled there. Tom was born in the Sussex village of Angmering and, when he grew to a man, his gypsy blood had given him such a dark complexion that he was nicknamed 'Black Tom'.

The nickname could equally well have described some of Oliver's dealings. For all his renowned brilliance as a jockey and reputed generosity, he was imprisoned more than once for incurring bad debts and was said to be constantly on the verge of bankruptcy. When he stopped riding, he trained – both horses and local prize fighters. One account of his funeral claims that his dog was the only respectable figure present.

Oliver's racing record, however, bears the closest of scrutiny. His enormous skill in the saddle meant he could command fees which other jockeys could only dream about, and he conquered Aintree completely to win the Grand National on three occasions – Gay Lad in 1842, Vanguard the following year and Peter Simple ten seasons later. But he became very much a Cheltenham local, living in a thatched home just outside Prestbury, and he was widely idolised for his vivid personality as much as his obvious talent.

There are endless stories about Tom Oliver. Once, it is said, he was riding in a chase at Warwick during a snowstorm. There were two circuits of the course to complete and so, confident in the belief that no-one in the stand could see much through the snow, he stopped his horse first time round and took shelter behind a hayrick. As the toiling field loomed up again, several minutes later, Oliver remounted and rejoined the race – in the lead, of course.

He once sold a horse of dubious character and, curious, asked the new owner what he intended to do with him. On being told that the horse would be used to pull the mailvan to the villages of Winchcombe and Toddington, Oliver said, 'Sir, you just give him a flick with the whip when you reach the Rising Sun pub on Cleeve Hill, and he'll kick you into Winchcombe post office.' It was a prophetic warning, for only a few weeks later the rogue animal kicked the mail van to pieces and took an early retirement from post-office duties.

Oliver had no regard for Victorian class distinction. He would not pander to owners, no matter what their social standing, and when one nobleman asked him his view of the best distance for his horse, Oliver replied: 'Your horse can stay four miles, but he needs a hell of a long time to do so.'

One of the great credits against Oliver's name is that he passed on much of his riding skill to another Cheltonian, George Stevens, who was to surpass even his tutor's remarkable Aintree achievements by winning the National five times between 1856 and 1870. On each triumphant occasion, his fans back in Cheltenham lit bonfires on Cleeve Hill to celebrate.

Stevens was born in 1833, the same year as Adam Lindsay-Gordon came into the world, far away in the Azores. Two apparently unconnected births – but two lives which were to become intertwined before, within the space of twelve months, both ended in tragic circumstances.

Lindsay-Gordon was one of the founder pupils at Cheltenham Boys' College but, despite an aptitude for poetry, he became much more fond of sport than learning. At the age of fifteen he was taught to ride by a livery keeper in Cheltenham named George Reeves. Soon his style was being polished up by Tom Oliver who, at about the same time, was perfecting the Stevens' skill. Oliver gave both men rides, Stevens as a professional and Lindsay-Gordon as an amateur. He also found in Lindsay-Gordon an enthusiasm for boxing and, after suitable training, he put him up for fights in some of the saloons which were prevalent around Cheltenham at the time. There was regular boxing in Prestbury itself, and at the Roebuck Inn, in the Old Town.

Lindsay-Gordon immortalised one of the earliest Cheltenham chasing courses in rhyme. His poem *How We Beat The Favourite* described a race run on a natural course at Noverton, a hamlet just across the Southam road from Prestbury village. The fences sound more formidable than even the stiff Prestbury obstacles of today; at least one was a stone wall! Adam's father lectured at Cheltenham College but, anxious to wean Adam off his sporting obsessions, decided his son should further himself in Australia. So he was packed off, a reluctant emigrant. He wrote more poetry down under, and rode more races. In fact he became Australia's champion amateur jockey, but life in the Antipodes clearly did not suit him. On 24 June 1870 in the scrubland of Brighton, South Australia, Adam Lindsay-Gordon shot himself.

If news of that suicide caused mourning among friends back in Cheltenham, worse was to come for the close-knit racing community which had grown up in Prestbury. On the second day of June the following

25 Priory Street, Cheltenham – the boyhood home of Adam Lindsay-Gordon.

year George Stevens, then thirty-eight, was riding his hack up Cleeve Hill to his cottage home when the most freakish of accidents cost him his life. A gust of wind lifted Stevens' hat off his head and so alarmed the horse that he turned and bolted back down the hill at fearsome speed. Stevens was not a man easily removed from the saddle, as his Aintree exploits will bear witness, and he was still intact, if not totally in control, when the frightened horse stumbled over a drainpipe near the foot of the hill.

Emblem Cottage, Cleeve Hill, George Stevens' home named after the second of his Grand National winners (1863).

IN MEMORY OF
GEORGE STEVENS
THE RIDER OF THE WINNERS
OF FIVE GRAND NATIONAL
STEEPLECHASES WHO, AFTER
RIDING FOR TWENTY YEARS
WITH NO SERIOUS ACCIDENT
WAS HERE KILLED BY A FALL
FROM HIS HACK ONLY THREE
MONTHS AFTER RIDING
"THE COLONEL" IN THE
GRAND NATIONAL OF 1871.

The plaque commemorating George Stevens.

Stevens was thrown and, as he fell into the gutter, his head crashed against a stone. Help was quickly at hand, and willing arms bore the fallen hero into a nearby farmhouse. But Stevens never recovered consciousness, and died the following day. He had never fallen in fifteen Grand Nationals, but a bizarre sequence of events only a few hundred yards from his home had ironically cost him his life. The place where he fell is still marked by a plaque, standing at the side of the hill where the road forks to Southam.

So by a combination of mischance and misery, Tom Oliver outlived both his distinguished pupil jockeys. Oliver spent his final days in Wroughton, another training centre of the day, near Swindon, and he died in 1874. But twenty-five years earlier, back in Prestbury, Oliver had been best man at the wedding which was to become perhaps the most significant in the town's racing history. It was the marriage of William Archer, son of a local livery man, and Emma Hayward, daughter of a pub landlord. For racing folk it was a marriage blessed in heaven for the pub, which became the couple's home, was the King's Arms in Prestbury, subsequently to become synonymous with the sport as a focal point for the town's training and riding fraternity.

The pub remains in place and, although it has long since become a steak bar, racing atmosphere a thing of the past, a plaque still stands on the wall in memory of William and Emma's most famous son, the five-times Derby winner Fred Archer.

William himself had been no slouch on a horse. He apparently had his first ride in a hurdle race during a meeting at Elmstone Hardwicke, near Cheltenham, when he was only nine years old. He ran away from home at fourteen, and finished up in Russia as jockey and stud-manager to Tsar Nicholas I, who paid him the then princely retainer of £100 a year. But he came home to find his bride and settle down to have a family. The breeding, as one might expect, was strong on good racing blood. But the strain of tragedy which seemed to infiltrate Cheltenham's racing folk so regularly during the nineteenth century, returned to claim two of their three sons.

Fred Archer was the sporting sensation of his day, a figure every bit as famous as Lester Piggott a century later and, it seems, similar in habit. The King's Arms plaque says he trained on 'toast, Cheltenham water and coffee' which, if you throw in a liberal supply of good cigars, is not so far removed from the Piggott diet. Like Lester, Archer made an early start to his racing career and was in the winner's enclosure at the age of twelve – although that event, a donkey race run in the paddock of the Plough Inn at Prestbury, will probably be hard to find in the form book. Dedicatedly restricting his weight, Archer became a truly great flat-race jockey and was champion by the time he was seventeen. The Epsom

Fred Archer spent much of his boyhood in Prestbury where his parents ran the King's Arms.

Derby became almost his personal benefit but there were many other big-race wins and, if legend is to be believed, the occasional betting coup. One such windfall apparently brought Archer such a sum that he was able to buy the Andoversford Hotel for his parents.

If Archer was the Piggott of his generation, he had to do without all the modern advantages of private planes and chauffeurs. Fred travelled everywhere by train, clocking up a phenomenal amount of journey miles.

Although flat racing had disappeared from the Cheltenham area, Archer continued to live in Prestbury. To quote the plaque again: 'The shoe of his pony hangs up in this bar, where they drank to his prowess from near and from far.' Success and adulation did not bring Fred Archer happiness, however. When he was only twenty-nine and champion jockey for the thirteenth consecutive season he died tragically in the same way that Adam Lindsay-Gordon had chosen some fifteen years earlier.

The other two Archer brothers, William and Charles, became jump jockeys, and both enjoyed some success in the meetings which were held at various venues in the area. Prestbury Park had temporarily closed its doors to racing but other landowners filled the breach and steeplechasing became a gypsy sport, taking its tents and its trapping around the Cotswolds. Kayte Farm, in Southam, staged some meetings but, in 1866, the grandstand which had been erected there collapsed disastrously. The two hundred spectators who had been race-watching from the stand fell into the refreshment room below. Miraculously, no-one was killed. But plenty were injured, the organisers of the meeting were sued and costs of around £2,500, a staggering amount so long ago, were awarded.

Both William and Charles Archer were engaged to ride in the Cheltenham spring meeting of 1878. The most important event was still the Grand Annual Chase and the King's Arms should have been throbbing with family celebrations the night Charles brought home the coveted trophy. Instead, they were in mourning, for on the same day brother William had been killed by a fall in a hurdle race. He was probably not the first and certainly not the last rider to be killed in a fall at Cheltenham but, for the grieving locals, it was another of those most cruel bereavements, another of their own taken.

Charles Archer remained to perpetuate the family. He married and had a son, named Frederick after his elder brother. Frederick delighted those who yearned to see the Archers continue in racing, and trained the 1925 Grand National winner, Double Chance. His namesake, his lost uncle,

St George's Cottage, Cheltenham, birthplace of Fred Archer.

lived on – not least in the memory of the Cheltenham people – and the house where Fred Archer lived until the age of three, became something of a local shrine to his revered riding record. Not long ago, however, the house was burgled and most of the Archer mementoes, valueless in all but nostalgia, were taken.

Racing had begun to lose its attraction around Cheltenham as the nineteenth century neared its close. Although Francis Close had died, and with him the fervour of his followers, the sport appeared to have lost its way. It had no regular home and so no firm identity in Cheltenham. The Grand National remained a major sporting occasion, as it has ever since, but other jump meetings became more spasmodic and less well supported all around England, and there seemed a real, unthinkable danger that the sport would suffer a slow but inevitable death by disinterest.

That fate was avoided by the sale of Prestbury Park and the enthusiasm of its new owner, Mr Baring Bingham, to restore and re-establish the racecourse. He rebuilt the grandstand, erected rails around the course and then re-launched it upon the unsuspecting public with a meeting in 1898. It was no overnight sensation; the people of the area had become indifferent to the pleasures of the turf and needed to be weaned back onto them. But in relative terms, it was not a long process. A new age, the forerunner of the Cheltenham we know today, was about to dawn. In April 1902, over two days, the Cheltenham Festival was run at Prestbury Park for the first time.

It was not run on the grand scale of the 1980s, of course. Nor did the purses on offer remotely resemble a racing fortune. But there was good jump racing, there was gambling, there was drinking, and if the church had anything to say about it, their protests remain unrecorded.

I would not mind betting there were a few legless locals stretched across the pavements of Prestbury by nightfall. Probably plenty of monied visitors, perhaps even from overseas, leaving the course in their plush hansom carriages and going off in search of the best the town had to offer. The Festival, you see, has not changed much since then. It has just become bigger and better.

Chapter 2

THE OFFICES OF PRATT & Co., racecourse managers, take some finding these days. Leave the Brighton-bound M23, wind through some of Sussex's pretty, commuterbelt villages and then do battle with the Haywards Heath one-way system. Pratts have a shop-front window announcing them, on a hill just outside the town centre, and, most mornings, Bryan Robinson can be found upstairs, in a room surrounded by books and files which trace the business of many a racecourse back many a bygone year. Cheltenham has a cabinet to itself, which is perfectly proper considering the name of Pratts has been strongly linked with the course since the earliest years of this century.

Bryan Robinson is a burly man with a cheery, florid face and spectacles which give him a vague air not borne out by his manner. Someone told me he looks like Jorrocks, which he may or may not consider a compli-

ment. Everyone agrees that he must know more about the day-to-day running of the Cheltenham course over several decades than any man alive. Mr Robinson is senior partner of the company, a position previously held by his father, Ernest, until his death in 1953. Ernest Robinson had joined Pratts in 1911 and, when the Great War loosened its grip on the world and racing returned, he became clerk of the course at Cheltenham as it entered a proud new era.

Pratts themselves go back much further, to 1860 when John Pratt inaugurated the company. The business was set up in fashionable Mayfair and, under the trading name of Pratt & Barbrook, they performed the function now controlled by Weatherbys, taking entries for most English courses and several in Europe. Primarily, however, they were responsible for the efficient operation of a great many of the country's racetracks, supplying clerks to courses now long since extinct, such as Rugby, Kingsbury, Dover, Cardiff and Lambourn, as well as others, like Worcester, Ludlow and Devon & Exeter, which have survived the economy squeeze and still flourish today. In addition, they acted as handicappers and stakeholders, ran a sideline in horse insurance and were agents for various jockeys and trainers. In those days theirs was a business with tentacles throughout the racing industry, exercising a considerable degree of control.

Things are on a much smaller scale now, but back at the turn of the century, business was booming when John Pratt accepted Frederick Cathcart as an equal partner. Mr Cathcart was to become the first secretary of the Cheltenham Steeplechase Club and then, in 1908, chairman of the newly-formed Steeplechase Company.

This correctly suggests that the Cheltenham course was beginning to progress along more commercial lines and, in fact, the days of the rural racetrack and its amateur, strictly-for-fun supervision were gone forever. The town, and particularly Prestbury, continued to house a large number of trainers, and now they had a course which more than complemented their presence.

It is doubtful whether racing in Cheltenham has ever seen more exciting times. The slump was over, the sport was thriving and the course began to sprout new facilities at an even faster rate than the 1980s expansion.

With the far-sighted acquisition of the course by the Steeplechase Company, there were now no barriers, no dark shadows hanging over the

Opposite: *Bryan Robinson presents the Cathcart Challenge Cup to Fred Winter after Roller-Coaster won the race in 1979. Bryan Robinson always presents the trophy for this race which is named after Frederick Cathcart, first secretary of the Cheltenham Steeplechase Club.*

NEW RACE STAND.

CHELTENHAM NATIONAL HUNT RACE MEETIN

LUNCHEON AND PRIVATE VIEW TO PRESS AND OFFICIALS ON THE
COURSE, MARCH 6, 1911.

On horseback:—Mr. H. Fane Gladwin (steward).

Back row:—G. V. Bright ("Gloucestershire Graphic"), N. Bennett ("Gloucestershire Echo"), A. Holman (designer and builder of course), Philip M. Chance ("Gloucester Citizen"), —. Maylam (Messrs. Pratt's Inspector of Courses).

Front row:—Superintendent A. W. Hopkins (Cheltenham Police), H. W. Bennett ("Gloucestershire Echo"), F. H. Cathcart (Clerk of the Course), W. J. Crawford ("Cheltenham Looker-On"), R. Willett ("Birmingham Daily Mail").

future. Its most recent parallel is the Aintree saga and the years of doubt over the National course before the future of this piece of national heritage was secured in a way which brought relief to anyone who has ever sampled its unique atmosphere. So it was with Cheltenham. Racing in the parish had survived so precariously for so long that there was now an understandable urge to demonstrate the new stability in a concrete way. In May, 1908, a new members' stand was opened. The sun shone, spring was well advanced and the men wore their panamas and lightweight suits, the ladies put on their summer frocks and clutched their parasols while taking tea on the lawn. By today's standards it may not have been much of a grandstand – more on the lines of Stratford or

Opposite: *The members' stand, opened May 1908, and members' lawn.*

NATIONAL HUNT STEEPLECHASE MEETING IN CHELTENHAM.

BRILLIANT SCENES AND RACING WEDNESDAY MARCH 8 1911

Huntingdon than the Cheltenham mecca – but it was to see service for the next seventy years. Between 1908 and 1914, each new season saw another part of the building programme completed until, just as the place was ready to fulfil the dreams of innovators like Cathcart, racing was suddenly overtaken by bloodier battles.

The splendid facilities did not go to waste. Far from it. In October of 1914, with the war clearly set in for a lengthy stay, the Cheltenham course was turned over to the Red Cross as a troop hospital. The first patients were bedded down in the ladies' drawing room (one facility which has vanished with the years); the next batch were put in the luncheon rooms. The jockeys' dressing-room became a kit-room where the clothes of the patients were stored, and an office was set up in the weighing-room. The tasks of the administrators included the issue of five cigarettes per day to each patient but, if that was one of their luxuries, they did at least have some entertainment for racing continued at the track, albeit on an obviously reduced scale. There was a Boxing Day meeting in 1914 and six days of racing the following year. Entries were relatively small, crowd figures inevitably dropped, but the patients, those who were able, sat out on the balconies and the lawns drinking in one of the obstinately eccentric sights of wartime England.

When peace returned, and serious sport was restored to the calendar, it quickly became clear that the years of grief and misery had done nothing to dampen enthusiasm for racing. If anything, the opposite applied and with the natural euphoria of regained freedom, thousands flocked to Cheltenham for the spring meetings of 1919, only weeks after the last wounded troops had left their beds in the ladies' drawing-room.

Ernest Robinson took office as clerk of the course, though continued to live in the Reigate home which had been in the family for generations. Ernest's father, grandfather and great-grandfather had all been involved in racing as judges, but Ernest had been prevented from following family tradition by poor eyesight. Instead, he became one of the most influential course administrators in England, and succeeded to the position of senior partner at Pratts.

Robinson presided over the years which shaped Cheltenham's future. In 1923, the spring festival had reached such a peak of popularity that it was decided to extend it from two to three days. (It has remained at three ever since, despite the occasional clamour from various quarters to add on a fourth day.) Then, the following year, came the introduction of what was to become the premier steeplechasing classic, the Gold Cup, and in 1927 the parallel race for hurdlers, the Champion Hurdle, was added to the National Hunt meeting card.

Opposite: *National Hunt steeplechase meeting at Cheltenham, 8 March 1911.*

During the First World War the course was used as a troop hospital. Patients are seen here in the Cheltenham Ward which is now the Arkle Bar.

Although jump racing continued to come a poor second to the flat in the eyes of owners, trainers and public, and although prizes continued to be comparatively small, the main Cheltenham meeting now had an established niche and an enormous following. There was to be no looking back.

When the Second World War made its unwelcome entrance the course was once again used for the national effort, though this time as living and training quarters for troops waiting to be dispatched to the action. Those trainers who struggled on through the war years had something to aim at, for the Gold Cup was actually run in all but two seasons, the years of 1943 and 1944 when all steeplechase racing in England was cancelled. The festival meeting was trimmed back in terms of races programmed and cash offered, and when Davy Jones rode Red Rower to victory in the 1945 Gold Cup, he earned for his owners the comparative pittance of £340, less than half the winner's prize in 1924, when the race was first run, and considerably less than one per cent of the race's value when the 1980s dawned. That, however, was of minor consequence. At the time, the fact that the race could be run at all, that the course and most of its patrons had survived those terrible few years, was really all that mattered.

Anyway, prize money rapidly grew. In 1946 the Gold Cup purse more than trebled, to £1,130 and by 1952 it had exceeded £3,000 for the first time. More, and richer owners were being attracted to jump racing, crowds were on the increase, the boom years were underway. By some racing folk, whose blinkers allow them to see nothing outside the confines of the flat, the growth of jumping has passed unnoticed. There were many disbelievers, many more who did not want to believe, when Cheltenham was able to announce that its 1984 Festival was the richest three-day meeting ever held in the country, flat or jumping.

It was into the prospering post-war years that Bryan Robinson first launched his tentative racing involvement. His father was still clerk at Cheltenham and Bryan's earliest memories of the course paint a vivid comparison with the vastness and luxuries now on offer. 'In 1947,' he recalls, 'the only car park was much smaller than any one of the four we have now. The Festival had been postponed after some of the worst winter weather anyone could remember, but the main events were eventually held on a Saturday in April. It was the biggest crowd I had ever seen – about 36,000, they said – and it was a lovely summery day. But because of the war damage and the rebuilding there were no real facilities at all – no bars to drink in, and wooden huts for toilets.'

Mr Robinson never did become clerk at Cheltenham – a salaried partner at Pratts, Bob Wigney, took the job for six years after the death of Ernest Robinson – but he has been as close as anyone to the centre of the operation over the last thirty years and remains a director. Pratts managed the course until 1978 and still direct the staffing operations now. Their racecourse management business has contracted, so that they are now only in charge of the south coast courses Folkestone, Plumpton, Fontwell and Brighton, but Bryan remembers the days when, because he was expected to attend and supervise meetings at each of their courses, he literally used to get up in the morning not sure whether it was Monday and Plumpton or Thursday and Folkestone. Over lunch at Cheltenham one day he related how the merry go-round life once got the better of him.

'I had a regular routine. Up early, eat the breakfast which my sister would always produce, then dress and drive off to the day's meeting. This particular day, I couldn't understand why everything seemed so quiet when I came downstairs. It was also very unusual to find my sister not around, but I made do, prepared some breakfast for myself and, as the papers had not arrived, tried to remember which course I was to go to that day. I still wasn't sure when I had put on my suit, picked up my briefcase and opened the front door. It was only at that moment that I

This splendid horse-drawn ambulance was in use in 1912.

realised that my sister was sleeping in because it was Sunday and there was no racing.'

Bryan Robinson never misses a day's racing at Cheltenham, and hasn't done for many years. He drives up from Surrey, normally the evening prior to the meeting opening, and stays in his favourite hotel in Prestbury, dining well and sleeping soundly before entering into the fray the following morning. He admits to being more of an administrator than a racing enthusiast and, although he likes if possible to watch some of the major events, he rarely has the chance. He busies himself around the weighing-room, keeping a sharp eye open for anyone who may have slipped past the stewards to trespass where few are permitted. Then there are the presentations to supervise. 'So I don't get to see much racing,' he sighs, 'but I do occasionally go racing at courses which Pratts have nothing to do with, but even then what I most enjoy is the opportunity to pick holes in their administration. I never rode myself, you see,' he adds, glancing down at his ample figure in a self-explanatory way.

Just occasionally, however, the absent-minded streak shows through again. He cheerfully admits it. 'I woke up in the middle of the night once and thought I heard noises outside the bedroom. My immediate thought was that I had burglars, and I wondered how on earth they had got past my dogs, who always make a hell of a din if anyone comes near. I got out of bed, groped around to the door in the darkness, then went out in the corridor to confront whoever it was. As I stepped out, the door slammed shut behind me. I was in my hotel in Cheltenham, wearing only my pyjamas, and the "burglars" were two other guests returning from a late night out. Luckily, they were sober and helpful enough to go down-stairs and collect another key so that I could let myself back into the room.'

The handing-over of authority at Cheltenham, concluded when Race-course Holdings appointed their own full-time manager in 1978, might, one suspects, have come a little hard to Bryan Robinson, but he continues to work alongside the new, professional order, sometimes praising their enterprise and direction. Pratts lives on in Haywards Heath, its range now restricted and its image perhaps a little old-fashioned. But they, as a company, and Bryan Robinson, as a character, provide one of few remaining strands linking the elegant, aspiring Cheltenham of Victorian days, with the ebullient commercial vehicle which has come to live within the racecourse in the eighties.

In 1964, the Cheltenham course had limited assets and a great many headaches. There were fears that the land could be bought for building purposes. Soon there were to be rumours that Lord Wigg, chief of rac-ing's Levy Board, wanted to take the National Hunt festival to Sandown. It was a worrying time.

Into this confused picture emerged a steadying and enduring influence. A consortium was formed, named Racecourse Holdings Trust, and after relatively brief negotiations, they bought the Cheltenham course for what now seems the pittance of £240,000. Twenty years on, the Steeplechase Company at Cheltenham is showing a healthy surplus every year.

The man at the head of the Trust is John Henderson, father of race-horse trainer Nicky Henderson. Not that father was a great racing man who encouraged his son to follow him. Mr Henderson senior was a highly successful stockbroker and Nick spent six months in the city after leaving school, 'Fearing that my career had been mapped out for me. But it couldn't last – they would never have known what to make of me there.' So Nicky went into the racing game which had been of interest to his father as a socialiser, spectator and owner of flat horses ... until the Trust was formed and he found himself amongst the owners of the world's greatest jumping course.

'It was entirely financial reasons, rather than racing ones, which at-tracted me to the venture. I was a hunting man, and I used to go racing quite often, but I was not then a member of the Jockey Club.

CHELTENHAM POLO TOURNAMENT AT PRESTBURY PARK, JULY 1st, 1911.

FOUR CLUBS—WATERMOOR HOUSE, BEAUFORT, ARLE COURT, AND CLEEVE GRANGE—COMPETED FOR A SWEEPSTAKE. WATERMOOR HOUSE AND BEAUFORT TIED.

1.—A grand run down the ground by Beau- 3.—A strung-out field 5.—Mr. E. M. Munby (hon. secretary), on 6.—Watermoor House team: Messrs. P,

'Cheltenham had always been a country course, but its potential was obvious. What we have done is to secure its future and then establish a good, progressive team there to push ahead with expansion. We are a non-profit-making company. The shares are held by the Jockey Club and, once our salaried staff have been paid, every penny goes back into the courses we run.'

Those courses now make up an impressive list. Cheltenham was the first; the Trust then purchased Wincanton, another well-supported country course, for £54,000 and, since then they have added Warwick, Market Rasen, Nottingham, Newmarket, Haydock Park and, most recently, Aintree. The operation is now co-ordinated from a Portman Square office, near the Jockey Club itself, where ex-soldier Tommy Wallis heads a small staff looking after the day-to-day supervision of the courses.

'We don't get involved in their individual race-planning or their parochial problems,' explains Mr Henderson. 'We hold the purse strings and give each course an annual budget. They must not exceed that by more than £5,000 without coming to us. One of our most important tasks is to appoint the Board at each course. If we get the right men in charge, the place will run itself; if we don't, we are in for some troubles.'

John Henderson, who used to live in the hunting country of Northamptonshire and ride competently in point-to-points, is now based at Newbury, only a few miles from his son's stables but he keeps a flat in London and, despite his retirement from stockbroking, he retains directorships of a number of companies, including Barclays Bank. He keeps in touch with Tommy Wallis by telephone – 'he probably rings me four times a week, but more if there are problems' – and he attends the major meetings at each of the Trust's courses.

He was one of seventeen people who formed the Trust by putting up £100 each. They all eventually handed over these shares to the Jockey Club. He sees nothing unusual about the nature of his organisation, pointing out: 'Arnold Goodman once said that the marvel of England is the volunteer, and it is true. Just look at all the volunteers in racing, from the stewards through to the St John Ambulance staff.

'Cheltenham is thriving now because it has a viable vehicle in its Festival, and facilities in the Prestbury Suite which keep the course occupied throughout the year. I like to think it is well organised and a credit to us. The new stands have certainly helped, and there are two more building stages to come. We have been lucky with our chairmen, from John Willoughby de Broke to Miles Gosling. The right people have been in charge.'

Opposite: *For many years polo was played regularly at Prestbury Park and was very much a social event.*

RHT came into racing at just the right time, stabilising rocky courses in a tight financial period. They have achieved much elsewhere and will no doubt be the making of Aintree at the end of its survival saga. At Cheltenham they provided the security and the impetus for men like chairman Miles Gosling and manager Edward Gillespie to use their knowledge of the sport and their skill in business to such evidently brilliant effect. The Trust's directors stay largely unseen and wholly inconspicuous in the background because that is the way they like it. Most racegoers visiting Cheltenham have probably never heard of RHT and have no idea of their role, but the fact is that the course would certainly not be so successful, and might not even exist at all, but for their timely intervention two decades ago. Their part in the history of Cheltenham is not one which racing folk will discuss. But it is assuredly one that businessmen should admire.

Chapter 3

THE OLDEST CHELTENHAM HERO alive took a while to answer when I knocked on the solid timber door of his cottage. When he appeared, wrapped up in waistcoat and cardigan against the chill of the spring evening, his cheery apology explained he had just come in from working on the farm and had wanted to finish marking up the racing results off the radio. Tim Hamey had left behind his seventy-eighth birthday yet was continuing his life with the restless relish of a man half his age.

James Henry Hamey, renamed Jack on 1920s cigarette cards, 'Loopy' by at least one trainer and Tim by the rest of the racing world, rode a horse named Koko to win only the third running of the Gold Cup, in 1926. Fifty-eight years later, he stood on the members' lawn casting a critically approving eye over the triumph of Burrough Hill Lad. That 1926 race was both the first and last time he rode in the Gold Cup, yet he has been present at all but a handful of the subsequent runnings, first as a freelance jockey hoping for spare rides, then as a trainer with stables bordering the course and, finally, reluctantly, as what one might describe as just another racegoer if it was not for the fact that he is recognised and greeted by so many.

It grieves Tim to be on the outside of racing, looking in. Given his own way he would still be riding and training now. Until very recently, he still was. 'We ran out of horses about five or six years ago,' he said sadly. 'I miss them terribly, of course, but to do the job properly you have to ride out every day, and I probably couldn't do that anymore.' He in fact resigned himself to advancing years and the angina which bothers him when past the age of seventy, slipping lightly off a saddle for the final time and deciding he should start leading a relatively quiet life. 'I still go and work on the farms every day,' he stressed, as if I suspected him of decadent idleness. 'I wouldn't like to be at home doing nothing.'

Hamey was born in Grantham, something he shares with a lady who won another of our national institutions, and by the end of the First

Opposite: *Tim Hamey and Koko clear the last fence to win the Gold Cup in 1926.*

World War he was riding in Red Cross gymkhanas and winning pony races. He had grown up with horses, as his father broke them in for a business, and at fourteen he left school and went to start an apprenticeship with a local trainer.

'I went through three lots of apprenticeship. The first trainer retired, the second went broke and the third, in Newmarket, I hated so much that I walked out after a month. It didn't put me off, though. I knew I could ride, and when I had my first winner, on the flat at Leicester, I beat the great Steve Donoghue by a short-head.' He had one more flat winner, this time by a neck from Donoghue's brilliant contemporary Charlie Smirke. 'But I began to get too heavy when I was sixteen, so I went jumping,' he explains. It was a move he never regretted.

He recalls his early races over obstacles as if they happened last week, instead of more than sixty years ago. 'My first ride was over fences, in a three-mile chase at Birmingham. It was on a horse called Castle Robin and I got round, which was the main thing. Then, two or three weeks later I rode my first winner, in a hurdles race at Market Rasen.'

The riding career of T. Hamey was related at a gallop, the narrator occasionally screwing up his still handsome face or poking the fire contemplatively as he wrestled with a name or a year. While Tim perched on the edge of an armchair in the sitting-room of the seventeenth-century beamed cottage his wife Phyllis sat a few feet away on the sofa, occasionally interrupting his flow with memories of her own. Like the day they met each other: 'Tim invited himself to tennis at my family's house,' she revealed with a prim pull of her dark shawl around her shoulders. Or the horse called Chain Link which Tim trained to win thirteen races: 'He used to drink the milk my cows gave. What a character he was! We sold him but nobody else could handle him so he came back . . . he kicked the wall down once.'

But Phyllis had jumped a few years. Tim was back on horseback, in the years leading up to his greatest triumph.

'I had a retainer with a stable which moved to Newmarket. I went with them, but they were cutting out the jumpers so I came back to live in Cheltenham and picked up the pieces as a freelance. I was only eighteen but I had a place to live, in Bishops Cleeve, and I got by all right, often going to the races without a ride and picking up three or four spares. It was like that in those days – a lot of trainers just wouldn't bother to book their jockeys in advance.'

Tim's earliest memory of Cheltenham, however, was a comical one. While still living in his native Grantham, he had ridden a winner at Haydock Park. The owner of the horse wanted to run him again in the imminent meeting at Cheltenham, booked Hamey for the ride and instructed him to go down on the train with the horse and then instal him in the racecourse stables for the night before the race. This, for a teenager, was quite a proposition: 'We arrived at Lansdown Station and I asked the way to the racecourse. I was told it was easy – just follow the tramlines. There were no horseboxes in those days, so I got on board the horse and rode him, at a walk, all the way up the Promenade. It was early closing day and, with all the shops closed, their doors and windows acted like one long mirror and I watched myself riding this racehorse up the shopping street. It was a strange experience. We got to the stables eventually, and I booked in at the Royal Oak pub nearby. I'd never seen the Cheltenham course, never even been to the place before, but as we had won from the front at Haydock I tried to make all again when the race got underway. It didn't work – the horse put his feet in the hurdle next to the old polo stand and dropped me into the gorse. I was pulling thorns out of my backside for weeks afterwards, so I had good reasons to remember Cheltenham!'

Five years later, Irish businessman Frank Barbour asked Tim to ride his horse in the Gold Cup. Koko was unfancied, at least by the average punter, and started at a generous 10-1 in a field of eight. But his jockey had very few doubts he would win. 'Koko was a front-runner, a bold jumper who loved to lead throughout. So I jumped off in front and made all, always confident we would win. We had no problems at all and won by four lengths. It could have been more.'

His main impression of the course at that time is that 'It was like a saucer – there was no straight and you had to go round on one leg'. But it didn't bother him that day. Tim Hamey was the toast of Bishops Cleeve, and in years to come he became one of the busiest, if not most glamorous jockeys of his era. Forty winners was his best return for a season but, considering the comparative scarcity of good rides for freelances, this represented an impressive performance.

A few weeks after winning the Gold Cup, Tim had his first Grand National ride, again on Koko. This was not so successful, as the horse fell at Bechers on the first circuit, but it began an unbroken sequence of twelve National rides which were to give Hamey some of the best and worst memories of his career.

He won the race in 1932 on Forbra, owned by a Ludlow bookmaker, and the commemorative linen poster, tracing the winner's pedigree and detailing its connections on the great day, still hangs on a wall in the Hamey home. In another room, however, hangs a photograph of a horse called Grakle which prompts a less triumphant tale. The character of Grakle can be gathered from the fact that he gave his name to the cross noseband which was first used to restrict his wayward tendencies. Hamey recalls the unfortunate experience of a jockey called Eric Foster, with whom Grakle ran off the course at Ludlow and into the shopping streets of the town. Although Tim did not have quite the same trouble with the horse when he rode him at Aintree, Grakle did make a spirited effort to run out on passing the stands, and it was only the Hamey horsemanship and the rails which kept him on course for a clear round.

Two years on, Grakle was being aimed at Liverpool again and Hamey was to have the ride. This part of the plan came to grief in the National Trial at Newbury, in which Grakle's jumping let him down and Hamey was taken to hospital for stitches in his head. 'I haven't been right since,' he jokes, 'but the worst of it was, I lost the ride in the National. The owner thought I had no chance of being fit in time so he engaged someone else to ride. I recovered, rode something else in the race, and Grakle won without me. At least the owner didn't forget – he sent me that photograph and £50 as a consolation present. It was a lot of money then.'

Amazingly, for one who rode so many years, Tim was never again confined to hospital by a fall. There were times, however, when he should have been, such as the day when he broke his collar-bone in the Scottish Grand National. 'I didn't want to see a doctor up there so I got on the night-train from Bogside, which reached Cheltenham at six o'clock the next morning. By the time I got off, the shoulder had been jogged around so much by the train that I was in agony.'

He started training in Bishops Cleeve in 1938 but this new career was barely out of its infancy before the war. Tim joined the army, and served for three-and-a-half years in Egypt, while Phyllis worked at home for the Ministry of Labour, and when the war ended they tried to pick up the threads. 'It was hard work, starting up all over again, but we found a nice place at Prestbury, just on the bottom end of the course, and I trained there for twelve or thirteen years. There were a lot more trainers in Cheltenham at that time – it was very much a racing community, like Lambourn is today, and most of us were based around Prestbury. We mostly got on well together, and there was a friendly relationship between the local trainers and the racecourse. They often called me in to pass an opinion about the siting of a fence, and I even lent them some of my horses to try out the new course which was being built just after the war.'

Eventually, and with great irony, it was the course itself, and its perpetual expansion, which drove Tim Hamey away. In 1958, Bryan Robinson told him that his land was needed for widening the new course. They wanted to knock down his house and stables, turf the land, put part of a racetrack where once there had been racehorses at rest. It was a compulsory purchase which Hamey took with good grace. 'Mr Robinson was very good to me. He gave me time to look around for another place, and we finally found one. I was sorry to go but there was nothing to be done about it.'

36

The Hameys moved to the village of Whaddon-with-Brookthorpe, near Gloucester, and still live there today. For some years, they carried on training, handling such locally-named horses as Whaddon Green and Whaddon Hero, but the operation gradually wound down, rather faster than did Tim's fascination for the racing game. That is still very much in evidence, and it is a rare raceday at Prestbury if he cannot be found, on the lawn or outside the weighing-room, in session with his cronies and contemporaries. Tim will doubtless be reminiscing about long-forgotten courses like Cardiff, Manchester and Gatwick – he rode winners at them all – or about the time when an owner contacted him in the Channel Islands with instructions to get to the west of Ireland by the following day for a ride in the Galway Plate. That won, too. Phyllis, perhaps, will retell the story of the 2 am phone call which told her that Tim had been killed. 'I'd have believed it,' she giggles, 'except for the fact that he was lying in bed next to me.'

Phyllis's favourite tale is of the time her geese escaped onto the course at Prestbury and followed the horses round in a hurdle race. Tim would rather talk of great bygone jockeys, men like F.B. 'Dick' Rees – 'the greatest jockey I've seen; he could lift a tired horse, and he showed me up a few times' – or maybe the two riders everyone seems to mention as a pair, Billy Speck and Billy Stott.

Michael Scudamore, that great jockey-turned-trainer, passed on a story of the day Speck and Stott turned up to ride at one of the London tracks in dinner suits. They had been on the town all night, but as Scudamore says: 'It made no difference to them, they were such fine riders.'

Speck and Stott were neighbours in Bishops Cleeve, and great socialites together despite varying tastes. One drunk little else but tea and smoked incessantly; the other could take a prodigious amount of champagne before sobering up almost instantly. 'He had the cure,' says Tim Hamey with a wicked smile of memory. 'It was Lea and Perrins sauce.'

They were first and second in the 1933 Gold Cup, Stott partnering Dorothy Paget's magnificent Golden Miller to the second of his five successive wins in the race, Speck finishing ten lengths adrift on Thomond II. Two years later, the horses clashed in the race again. This time, the ride on Golden Miller went to another Cheltenham-based jockey, later to train, Gerry Wilson. But Speck was again on Thomond and this time it was a battle worth travelling hundreds of miles to see. Tim Hamey was in the stands that day and recalls: 'It was a privilege to watch it. The two horses drew right away from the field on the second circuit and raced neck-and-neck all the way round. They landed together over the last and it was a very close thing which one won. It was the greatest race I've ever seen, and Golden Miller should be ahead of Arkle in my book.'

The winning distance was three-quarters of a length. Poor Thomond

The Hon. Dorothy Paget leads in Golden Miller (Billy Stott up) after his second Gold Cup win (1933).

was second again, and Billy Speck was destined never to get another chance of winning the great race. A month later, at Cheltenham's April meeting, the Prestbury patrons witnessed another of the tragedies in their course's history when Speck was killed in a fall.

'He was the best, most intelligent race-rider I ever saw,' says Tim Hamey. 'He used to weigh up every single horse in the race, his chances, the way he was likely to run, everything about him. I can still see him now, sucking in his cheeks as he always did, and telling me if he thought my horse had a chance. He was a great man, and a great jockey.'

If Hamey, Speck and Stott conjure colourful memories from the Festival's earliest years, no name is more evocative of Cheltenham's past nor, incidentally, more concerned with its present and future, than Nicholson. To be more accurate, perhaps Nicholson should be coupled with Holman, for it was the marriage of 'Frenchie' Nicholson and Diana Holman which linked a great racing man with a great Cheltenham family and, indirectly, spawned a fund of successes and stories of which the area would otherwise have been deprived.

It was in 1834 that William Holman came to Cheltenham and founded his dynasty. He rode the winner of the Grand Annual Chase no less than five times, then trained three winners of the Grand National. In between times, he produced six sons, of whom five were race-riding at one time. The most successful was George, who emulated his father by winning five Grand Annuals and was also a close second in the 1870 Grand National won by that favourite son of Prestbury, George Stevens. Of George Holman's brothers, William became secretary of the Cheltenham races in the 1860s and Alfred, having helped in the laying out of the current course, was jointly responsible for introducing the National Hunt Festival meeting. Frederick had a stud farm across the Evesham road from Prestbury Park, roughly where one of the course car parks is sited today. He had a good stallion named Petronel and, in the 1880s, charged the extravagant sum of two guineas for each mare sent to him.

'Frenchie' Nicholson – winner of the 1942 Gold Cup on Médoc II, Prestbury trainer, and famous for his 'jockeys' academy'.

Frederick's granddaughter is Diana Holman, who plays a significant, wide-ranging role in the Cheltenham story, largely, but not entirely, through her choice of husband. She still lives in Prestbury and, during the months in which this book was written, she paid twice-daily visits to the nursing home at which 'Frenchie' had been confined by illness. Mrs Nicholson's memory is clear and long, and her first recollections of the Cheltenham course go back to the pre-war days when polo was played in the centre.

Her father was a horse dealer and, chiefly because Cheltenham housed 'the best polo grounds in the west of England', he specialised in polo ponies during each summer and hunters every winter. The family lived on the perimeter of the racecourse and the stables attached to the house have only recently been pulled down to accommodate property development which most locals of any age consider an unseemly sort of progress.

Back in the 'thirties, however, Diana and brother Ron had no complaints about their Cotswold existence. As she recalls: 'Life inevitably revolved around horses, but there was plenty of variety. I learned to play polo, I hunted three or four days a week in the winter, and both Ron and I rode in point-to-points ... I always had the left-overs, though, because Ron said he was furthering his career if he rode a few winners. He went into the Army as a regular soldier and later won two Gunner Gold Cups at Sandown.

'Our involvement in racing was relatively small at the time, but for many years father provided the starter's hack for each Cheltenham meeting. I suspect his "payment" was the badges for my mother and me to go onto the stands. Living so close was a great advantage, of course, and even when the place was very packed for a big meeting we were home and having tea before most people had struggled away from the course.'

The Holmans retained a few racehorses in their yard, chiefly trained for friends, and towards the end of the 'thirties they began to make the annual pilgrimage to Devon for the August holiday meetings at Haldon, Newton Abbot and Buckfastleigh. 'The fields were generally small and, because the meetings were close together, the horses used to stay down for a week or more and maybe run two or three times. If you had anything that could gallop and jump you were virtually bound to win a race.'

It was on one such summer sojourn in Devon that Diana met 'Frenchie'. The liaison was not immediately popular with the Holman family, for reasons of a social taboo which would nowadays seem laughable but were then taken extremely seriously. 'In those days,' explains Diana, 'you just didn't marry jockeys. They were always given the social class of servants so, at first, things were pretty difficult for us. All the family came round to the idea eventually, though, and we were married in 1938.'

This was the year that 'Frenchie' rode perhaps the greatest of all Cheltenham horses, Golden Miller, already winner of five Gold Cups and now, with his fifth different jockey, going for a sixth. He failed heroically, going down by two lengths to the younger Morse Code and being cheered all the way back to the unsaddling enclosure. For Nicholson it was a brief and frustrating partnership – but it was not the last he was to see of Golden Miller's owner, the redoubtable Dorothy Paget.

Diana and Frenchie went to live in Epsom, and might have stayed there but for the ferocity of wartime. Some of the bombs meant for London found their way onto the downs instead and the Nicholsons quickly decided this was no place for a young married couple, quite apart from the baby boy who had come into the world ten days after the 1939 Gold Cup. They moved back to Lake Street in Prestbury, and stayed there for the next forty years, the Nicholson establishment becoming an institution known around the racing world.

The war had to be dealt with first, however and for those left to eke out a living from racing, the hardships were severe. Frenchie was turned down by the active services on medical grounds, despite trying every route to acceptance, so he joined the Cheltenham platoon of the Home

40

Guard in which, it seems, he gave very passable impressions of Clive Dunn's Corporal Jones in *Dad's Army*. Diana explains: 'They were drilled in the local women's institute headquarters and Frenchie was hopeless. He didn't know his right foot from his left, and he was forever dropping his rifle!'

'We continued to farm and we still kept a few horses. But with so little racing, Frenchie had very few rides. Just occasionally, there was a good day. I remember Windsor staging a meeting with about a dozen races on the card and Frenchie had eleven consecutive rides. I mixed brandy and egg in a bottle and gave him a little between races to keep him going.'

The best day of all was 21 March 1942 when Frenchie won the Gold Cup in what was to be the last running of the race until the war ended. Fog shrouded the course all day long and, although it was a Saturday, the crowd was small, the atmosphere eerily empty. Nicholson's mount was Médoc II, second favourite in the twelve horse field, but as the leaders raced to the top of the hill for the final time it seemed that Solarium and Broken Promise had the Cup between them. It was at the last open ditch,

Prince Regent ridden by Tim Hyde and trained by Tom Dreaper (who later trained Arkle) after his win in the 1946 Gold Cup.

only a few short yards from the Nicholson home in Lake Street, that fate took a hand. Both the leaders came to grief and Médoc, sufficiently far behind to avoid interference, was able to pick his way through the carnage and forge on to victory.

'Frenchie got a £100 present from the owner, Lord Sefton, and thought it was a great deal of money,' relates Diana. 'In those days, if you got £25 for a winner it was a decent present.'

Three years later, Nicholson shared the jockeys' championship with Fred Rimell, although racing was still so scarce that his tally of winners was a mere fifteen. Four of those came on one day, in the February meeting at Cheltenham. Nicholson rode another four-timer on his home course in November the same year and he remains the only man to have performed the feat twice.

As a jockey's wife – and, moreover, one who attended racing – Diana seems to have had the ideal temperament: concern without panic. 'I used to jump every fence with him and knew instinctively when his horse was wrong, but I never got in a state of worry. In fact I became much more nervous at racing when watching the horses we trained.'

For some years, Frenchie combined the jobs of jockey and trainer, an equation which many have attempted but few have solved. Within the limits of his comparatively small stable, however, Nicholson managed the operation with some success, though much credit for this was due to the unassuming versatility behind the scenes of his wife. 'I did all the office work, but not very brilliantly – my filing system would have baffled most secretaries. Every morning I led the horses at work, just as I had previously done for my father, and when we went racing I always drove the car because Frenchie hated it so much. I would saddle the horses when Frenchie was riding them, but I always thought the most satisfying part of my work was acting as nurse to the sick horses. I did all the bandaging and dressing and we had a dark ray lamp, which was unusual in those days, for the bad cuts.'

Nicholson never trained a Gold Cup winner but he did stable one. In 1948, the Irish trainer Vincent O'Brien sent horses to Cheltenham for the first time. Among them was Cottage Rake, winner of the Irish Cesarewitch the previous autumn and now aimed, with great confidence, at the chasing classic. O'Brien, later to switch with devastating effect to the training of flat horses, was reluctant to submit his star to the hectic bustle of Festival week in the racecourse stables, especially as security was nowhere near as tight as it is today, so he approached the Nicholsons, who agreed to have him in their yard. Diana recalls: 'Vincent gave us instructions to give the horse eggs and sloppy foods and just to keep him quiet. This was no trouble but, being as superstitious as most racing folk, I was alarmed when the owners arrived on the morning of the race and

The Vincent O'Brien-trained Cottage Rake is led in by his owner Mrs Vickerman after winning the 1949 Gold Cup – the second of his three wins.

had some pictures taken of the horse – something which is always supposed to bring bad luck. But they were fully confident, and quite rightly so as things turned out.' Cottage Rake won the Gold Cup three years in succession and, in 1949 and 1950, O'Brien also trained Hatton's Grace to win the Champion Hurdle. Both these horses now have bars named after them in the new members' stand, shrines to the talent of the great O'Brien, an Irish hero who is toasted time and again by his countrymen every March.

Through the late forties and fifties, Cheltenham remained a thriving training centre to complement the racecourse. Nicholson's reputation may be the most enduring, but his near neighbour John Roberts, who trained at the now demolished Prestbury Court, turned out the only local Gold Cup winner ever when Four Ten won the 1954 race. Gerry Wilson, who had ridden Golden Miller in one of his Gold Cup triumphs during the thirties, later took up training at Andoversford, just outside the town, and won a Champion Hurdle. Even the Piggott family, famous these days only for flat-race feats, were then widely represented in Cheltenham. Charlie Piggott, Lester's great-uncle, trained on Cleeve Hill and had fourteen winners on the local course. Keith Piggott also trained a few Cheltenham winners, including a horse called Mull Sack in the 1954 Festival – ridden by nineteen-year-old Lester.

But it was in Prestbury itself that the real racing atmosphere existed, especially during the nightly pub debates. Roberts was a regular at the Archers' old pub, the Kings Arms, but Nicholson remained faithful to The Plough until the management committed what, in his eyes, was the crime of starting to sell spirits as well as beer. He considered the pub spoiled, and took his custom elsewhere. Frenchie, it is said, could never sleep properly without supping his two pints of beer – never less and seldom more. His social routine was strict to the point where the landlord knew precisely when he was expected each evening, and Frenchie did not appreciate diversions from the schedule. He ran a horse in the Grand National one year which was not entirely unfancied, but Frenchie apparently told everyone who asked: 'I shall leave the course at 3.30 whether we win or not. I will drink in the Plough, as usual, not with these sharks.'

Frenchie and Diana lived at Lake Street, trained their horses and watched the racecourse at the end of the garden grow into a marvellous sporting monster. Their fortunes wavered, in the fashion of all but a lucky few trainers, and there were times when they had only a few horses left to look after. But two things kept them busy. The first was the unexpected arrival in the yard of Dorothy Paget's expensive string of jumping horses.

The Hon. Dorothy Wyndham Paget was much maligned and, very probably, much misunderstood. She was the second of five daughters born to Lord Queensborough, whose one aim in life seems to have been a son and heir and who, apparently, did not take kindly to failure in this department. Some of his sourness transmitted itself to his daughters and Dorothy, despite inheriting vast family wealth and wanting for nothing in the material sense, evidently found little fulfilment in life, outside the self-satisfaction of backing her own horses with quite ruthless courage.

By the time her horses came to the Nicholsons she had won no fewer than seven Gold Cups and four Champion Hurdles. In her thirty-year period of racehorse ownership, ended by her death when still relatively young, she led in the extraordinary total of sixty-eight winners at Cheltenham. She employed a variety of trainers during that time, more than one of the associations ending in bitter recriminations, so the Nicholsons might have been excused mixed feelings over the blessing of her undoubtedly lucrative custom. They were, however, an open-minded couple and they took up what was clearly as much an initiative test as one of training.

'It kept us on our toes,' explains Mrs Nicholson. 'We knew only her reputation when she sent her horses to us. Plenty of people thought she was crooked but I came round to believing that was an attitude born of jealousy in some minds, and lack of understanding in others. Certainly she was unlike any other owner we dealt with, and I can't deny that some of her ways were eccentric.

'In all, we had thirty of her horses. Some of them were quite useless, but she refused to sell them just in case someone else happened to win a race with one of them. Certain of the other horses, though, were high class, and we were able to win some valuable races for her.

'The routine was always the same before a race. In order that she could accurately assess the size of her bet, we had to give her a comprehensive breakdown of every runner in the field. Nowadays, the overnight declarations would make this relatively straightforward but at that time one never knew exactly which horses were running until forty-five minutes before the race. As Miss Paget seldom came racing herself, this involved me in queuing for the public phone box on the course in order to give her the information or, to be more accurate, to give it to her secretary, Miss Williams. In all the years we trained for her, I never once spoke to Miss Paget herself on the phone; all the business was conducted, very efficiently, by Miss Williams.'

In addition to assessing the other runners in each race involving a Paget horse, the Nicholsons were required to guide their owner in the critical matter of her betting. 'She never minded if we advised her not to have a bet,' recalls Diana, 'though I shudder to think what would have happened if one of the non-betting horses had then won. Fortunately, it never happened. If we thought her horse had at least an each-way chance in the race, we were to tell her the degree of her bet. The biggest bet of all was what she called a "banco". She had quite a few of those.'

'Miss P', as she was widely referred to in racing circles, invested £5 million in the purchase of horses. Nobody knows the extent of her investments with the bookmakers, and her appearance betrayed no such secrets. When she did leave her Buckinghamshire home to go racing – and such occasions were generally restricted to meetings at her favourite Windsor, or the most major of events such as the Cheltenham Festival

– she habitually wore a blue beret and an inelegant full-length brown coat which can have cost her no more than the loose change in her well-stocked purse.

In other ways, however, this mysterious woman, the first lady of steeplechasing for so long, was anything but mean. She sent expensive Christmas presents to everyone in the Nicholson yard and, when Frenchie's son David, by then a prominent jockey himself, organised a local raffle in aid of cancer research, she donated every one of the prizes, only insisting they were said to come from her greatest horse, Golden Miller.

If Dorothy Paget gave no more than a passing boost to the Nicholsons, they will forever be associated with the production line of jockeys which emanated from their headquarters. They became famous for the taking

At the age of sixteen David Nicholson's second ride over the Cheltenham obstacles resulted in a fall when he rode Keith Piggott's Royal Task in the County Handicap Hurdle 1956.

in of frail-looking boys with a passion to learn race-riding, and the ultimate dispatch of the completed article. Paradoxically, for Frenchie's life had been dominated by jump racing, the vast majority of their successes were flat jockeys.

There were two exceptions to this rule. The first was their own son, David, who must certainly be known as their earliest success, and the other was a tall intense young man who came to them as an amateur rider, eager to complete his education in the saddle. He was to go on to prominent things in later years, becoming one of the great heroes of Cheltenham in the spring of 1983. His name was Michael Dickinson. 'We didn't like taking on amateurs,' admits Mrs Nicholson, 'but there was something very different about Michael's attitude. He came here quite dedicated to learning and was very serious about the whole thing.'

David Nicholson's current eminence, training one of the largest strings of jumping horses in England, has been achieved despite suffering severely from asthma during his youth and early manhood. The problem is still with him to some degree, but totally under control when compared to the years when he could not walk any distance, or take any vigorous exercise, without seriously impairing his breathing. He went to school at Cirencester and Haileybury, chiefly because of their gravel soil which eased his condition, and although it did not prevent him from riding, he spent most of his leisure hours asleep.

His mother has a picture of David on a pony at the ripe old age of two-and-a-half. 'He could always ride,' she says. 'It came very naturally to him, and his nanny used to take him out on his pony, Snowy, rather than push him in the pram. He could ride racehorses at twelve and the asthma did not affect him in that at all. But it was a great worry. He was on a very restricted diet and often seemed extremely unwell.'

A Harley Street specialist was consulted. His investigations had shown there were thirty-two causes of asthma. David tried all manner of treatments before finally something was found which controlled, if not totally cured, it. He was able to take the same route as his father, riding successfully, then combining it with training, before concentrating on building his business at Condicote into a thriving, impressive yard.

David Nicholson played a significant part in the utterly accidental launch of his family's apprentices' academy. For when the diminutive figure of Paul Cook arrived on the Lake Street doorstep, eager to learn to ride, it was David who taught him. 'Horses ran for Paul,' says Diana, 'and when he looked like taking off as a jockey he was in no rush to leave us. Frenchie couldn't take him racing as he was too busy training the jumpers, so I took on the job, and it was then that it occurred to me we might make a side-line out of it. Frenchie and I discussed it, and it was agreed that it would become my business to run, although he would obviously do the actual coaching of any boys that came. At that stage, we certainly never imagined the idea would become quite such a success.

'I had never been flat racing much. Indeed, the only time I had even been to Newmarket was when I drove David to ride there when he was twelve. I remember thinking how small and fragile he looked to be up against all these comparative giants, but I was to grow accustomed to that feeling over all the years with the apprentices.'

Would-be jockeys were soon queuing up to come to the Nicholsons. 'We had dozens of applications and turned down some, because I can't work with people I don't like. The boys who did come became part of the family. It was a very personal thing for us, and I must say I enjoyed those years enormously.'

Although future stars of the racing game were soon commonplace at the academy, and obvious by their speed of progress, they were neither cosseted nor pampered. Quite the opposite. The Nicholson way was to ensure they grew up as rounded individuals, not just potentially high-earning sportsmen with inflated ideas. Frenchie, his sometimes gruff exterior guarding an essentially kindly nature, was the ideal man to mould them as they went about their daily work and, in their hours off the course or the gallops, Diana kept boredom, the greatest of all character killers, at bay by finding them a variety of ways to remain occupied. 'For instance,' she recalls now, 'they all had to dig the vegetable garden.'

The steady influx of apprentices meant that the Nicholsons only ever had to employ one full-time lad in their yard, spreading out the rest of the daily jobs among their brood. Deliberately, they discarded the idea of a hostel, reasoning that it was better for the boys to continue growing up in a family environment rather than being thrown together as a unit which could fracture into jealousies, homesicknesses and rebellions. So Diana cast her net around the Prestbury and Cheltenham area, finding each new apprentice a lodging with a family, very often on the council estates. 'The type of people they stayed with was more important than the standard of house,' she said.

Every boy taken on was told the ground rules. These included a ban on owning a car for the first three years of their stay, chiefly through the fear that it would breed laziness and produce excess weight which could abort all the efforts of the couple to turn out a saleable jockey.

Mrs Nicholson acted as chauffeur when the boys went racing, and did the job uncomplainingly throughout the years of the academy. She even enjoyed it. 'Some of the days were very long, and I think I got to know the routes to almost every racecourse in England. We might be heading for Catterick one day, Folkestone the next and Haydock the one after that, so I clocked up plenty of miles in a week. But, you see, I liked having the company of young people. They would have pop music playing on the car radio all the way up the motorway each day and I would learn all the latest songs. Then they would probably sleep all the way back again. But I think they kept me young, in a way.

'Discipline was seldom very difficult. We had to know what they were doing, of course, and there might have been the odd one who was a bit too boisterous. But I like to think we chose well, and those who spent any time with us knew they were here to learn, not to lark around.'

The telephone in the Nicholson's office became hotter over the years. Diana booked rides for all the apprentices and, as they included such talents as Pat Eddery, Tony Murray and Cook, all later to become top-class senior jockeys, the business prospered.

Meticulous attention was paid to detail in the education of a new boy. Any unfamiliar racecourse was walked before racing began, Mrs Nicholson herself usually accompanying the boy, and at home, Frenchie would advise, cajole and inspire with his words of wisdom.

On one auspicious day, no fewer than seven of the Nicholson apprentices were engaged to ride. Over the years twenty-five of them were to ride winners, an extraordinary testimony to the success of a quite unique racing establishment, especially as it was generally the small-time trainers, rather than their more illustrious colleagues, who provided the great majority of the rides for the rising stars of Prestbury.

Mrs Nicholson had always said she would retire from the exacting life of running the business and criss-crossing the country's motorway network, when she reached the age of sixty. She considered it would all become too much for her then. 'But Wally Swinburn, who was a great friend of ours in Ireland, got in touch and asked us to take his son. We did it as a favour to him but I am glad I stayed on to help him. Young Walter is, with the exception of Pat Eddery, the most natural jockey we ever had, and I am certainly proud of what he, and some of the others, have gone on to achieve.'

The Nicholson apprentices did not forget their mentor. In 1983, Frenchie's health was deteriorating rapidly and he was confined to a wheelchair. He still liked to go to race-meetings at Cheltenham, where he and his wife were now, quite properly, Life Members, and he would sit on the verandah of the weighing-room in between races, a figure inseparable from the history of the place. Eventually, however, he was admitted to a local nursing-home, where his visitors included academy old boys like Eddery and Cook. Diana Nicholson, now living in a bungalow in Prestbury village, tending the garden and occasionally glancing proudly at the yellowing old photographs of her husband on the wall, went to sit with him twice each day. But in April of 1984, Frenchie Nicholson died, and a little bit of Cheltenham died with him.

Chapter 4

AUTUMN SEEMED TO LAST forever in 1983. The mellow days of September, as green turned to brown, stretched on through October. November, traditionally bleak and forbidding, dawned unseasonally warm and, for once, Guy Fawkes parties were not ruined by rain. Umbrella salesmen were having a rough time, but the public was more cheerful than usual for the time of year. Racecourse administrators, however, found it hard to share the general enthusiasm.

Midway through the second week in November, Edward Gillespie gave a meaningful glare at the sunshine streaming through the window of his Cheltenham office and said: 'Lots of people keep telling me what wonderful weather we're having, but I don't notice it. All I know is that we could do with a couple of days' rain.' Across the room, seated at another desk behind a formidable pile of paperwork, Philip Arkwright nodded gloomily and picked up the telephone to make another optimistic call to the local weather centre, hoping for a hint of troughs moving in from the Atlantic. He was resignedly unsurprised to be told there was little chance of any measurable rain before the weekend.

It was the weekend which was bothering them. Major Arkwright, the clerk of the course, and Gillespie, the manager, were making final preparations for the twenty-fourth running of the Mackeson Gold Cup, and the weather was being distinctly inconsiderate. This was not the first racing of the season at headquarters. There had been three days in October, programmes in which the heavy artillery of trainers, having watched their small-time colleagues scrap over the August and September prizes on coastal and country tracks, announce themselves for the new campaign with a few, muscle-flexing runners. But the Mackeson is serious business, the first of the season's important, richly-rewarding chases and traditionally won by a horse likely to race for still greater glories in the months to come. The Mackeson is a major event in its own right, but it is also an overture in the jumping calendar, the lifting of the curtain for Act One in the play ... but it was so damned dry that the stars were likely to stay away, and the crowds with them.

Racing men are renowned for complaining about the weather. Invariably, it seems, things are not quite to their liking – the ground is too firm

Elain Mellor, champion lady jockey, dismounts from Ashlone after winning the Amateur Riders' Association NH flat race, 1983. Husband Stan, himself three times champion, trained the horse.

or too soft, the frost has stopped their horses working, the rain has come too soon, or too late. But a walk down the course at Cheltenham on that infuriatingly fine November morning was evidence enough that messrs Arkwright and Gillespie had reason for concern.

Foreman Phil Hatcher, a gentle giant of a man, was striding around in wellington boots, though the ground underfoot was such that he might just as well have worn sandals. 'If we had to race today, the going would be firm,' he reported. 'I am a bit despondent about it because there is really nothing to be done. We can't water the course at this time of year – it's physically impossible to get enough water all round and, even if we did, we'd be laying ourselves open to waterlogging when the weather does turn. We've put down sand on the take-off side of the fences and peat on the landings, so there shouldn't be too many complaints about that. But when the ground is as unyielding as this we just have to accept the fact that some trainers will not risk injuring their horses, however big the race. There is a long season ahead.'

He marched purposefully away into the crazy clutter of tractors, JCB's and rubble on the construction site of the new grandstand extension, due to be opened on the first day of the March Festival. It was reportedly on schedule and the builders, at least, were quite content for the sun to go on shining, even if everybody around them was scowling at the clear skies.

Phil Hatcher is in overall charge of the ground staff, which comprises thirteen full-time workers and upwards of thirty race-day casuals, including fence attendants, trained in safety measures, at every obstacle. Phil's working week is fully occupied with a hundred-and-one jobs around the vast acreage of the course but, on racing days, he supervises the operation on foot, carrying a radio so he can be summoned rapidly to any crisis around the course, and positioning himself by the invalids' stand during each race so he has the widest possible view of his domain. He lives in a bungalow at the top of the course and now plainly relishes the job, which he has done for ten years, and the sport itself. Strangely, however, he had been to only two race meetings in his life before joining Cheltenham, and admits even he had no conception of the backroom work which goes into the successful staging of a day's racing. 'The public,' he says, 'have no idea what goes on behind the scenes and it is best that they don't, because the only time they are likely to find out is when something goes wrong.'

If it could have been said things were going wrong at Cheltenham that morning, pretty much everything was right with the life of Jonjo O'Neill. The thirty-one-year-old Irishman was back on top of the jockeys' table after struggling for three years since badly breaking his leg in October of 1980. A naturally cheerful man, even his phlegmatic naure had been all but broken by the chain of events following his injury. He had tried to ride again too soon, aggravated the break and ended up flying to Switzerland for emergency treatment. Amputation was a sickening possibility and Jonjo, 'feeling lower than I've ever felt in my life,' was also in dire financial straits, having just bought a forty-five-acre farm on a budget which took no account of spending so many months out of work.

'I reached the stage where I didn't care what the doctors did to the leg so long as they stopped the pain,' he recalled later that day, standing on the wooden steps outside one of England's most rustic weighing-rooms

The O'Neill brothers – left to right *Jerome, Dennis, Thomas and Jonjo.*

and staring half-a-mile ahead to the hurdle on the far side of Bangor-on-Dee racecourse which had caused his fall. It was more than three years ago and his recovery was so triumphantly complete that he was on target to break his own record for the fastest fifty winners in a season, but the pain of the memory still flashed momentarily across his face. 'It was a hard struggle, getting rides back,' he explained. 'Most people believed I would pack up riding and I found I had a big psychological barrier to overcome. Even meeting people I knew well was difficult, because they all looked at me as if I'd come back from the dead. I had to start all over again and I probably made things even more difficult by setting out to prove things I didn't really need to prove. I take everything day by day now, never looking too far ahead and trying not to set targets.'

O'Neill, however, had driven down to the quaint, North Wales track – as different from Cheltenham's splendour as is possible to imagine – with the weekend on his mind, and a difficult decision to take of the sort which frequently confronts jockeys of his calibre. Should he spend Saturday at the Newcastle meeting, aiming to continue his splendid run of winners with five or six rides for his loyal northern trainers? Or should he go to Cheltenham and ride in the major event of the day. Was it to be quantity or quality? 'I've been offered the Mackeson ride on Pounentes,' he confided. 'It's a horse trained in Scotland by a man named Billy McGhie and I have already won on him a few times this season. He'll go well, he might even win – but I probably won't make up my mind where to go until Thursday night.'

Jonjo made his decision. He went to Newcastle for several fancied rides. He could have gone to Cheltenham and won the Mackeson Gold Cup.

Thursday morning at 10.45, and zero-hour approached. Philip Arkwright sat at his desk, the *Sporting Life* open in front of him. The next time his phone rang it would almost certainly be Weatherbys, ringing to read over to him the declarations for Friday's meeting. Although the Mackeson was still more than two days away, this would undoubtedly give an accurate guide to the way trainers were thinking and indicate whether many class horses were likely to be risked. It had still not rained, indeed the sun was shining obstinately, and there was a certain tension in the office.

'I've been out there again this morning,' said Philip, gesturing over his shoulder towards his course. 'And I've got myself into a state of thinking it's perfectly frightful. In fact with the sand and peat down it is probably not too bad – the horses will make a print, anyway. But the ground is officially firm.'

There was a steady stream of heads poked around the office door, chiefly staff with their own private troubles to solve. Elsie the cleaner, looking for all the world like Thora Hird playing a char lady, was anxious because the key to the ladies' toilet in the royal box did not fit. Paul Townley, the carpenter on Phil Hatcher's staff, was having problems with an advertising board and wanted to know if it would be considered indiscreet if it was hung on the guttering of the weighing-room building. The stewards, he was told, would not like the idea and there was a general feeling that such blatant commercialism would be thought 'the thin end of the wedge'.

At five to eleven, a smile appeared on the clerk of the course's well-bred features. 'The longer we have to wait, the more runners there are likely to be,' he explained. Two minutes later the phone rang and everyone was put out of their misery. Philip had hazarded a guess that the total number of declared runners for Friday's six races would be about thirty-five, and he was spot-on. 'It could have been worse,' he conceded as he surveyed his markings on the *Sporting Life* declarations page. 'But in two of the races, only two horses have been left in. What do we do if we have a non-runner in both those events – accept two walk-overs, or call in the local hunt for reinforcements?'

The medical facilities at Cheltenham are first rate – amateur Mr A. McTaggart receiving attention after a fall.

The morning reverted to type. Like any eve-of-meeting it was hectic, and while Philip left the office to go and compare notes with his foreman, manager Gillespie placated some anxious sponsors over the size of field for their race, touched up the chairman's speech for the Champion Jockey's Ball to be held at the course on Saturday night, checked that Paul Townley had coped with the placard problem and interviewed an applicant for an office job: all in the space of half-an-hour. He would not be stopping for lunch today.

Gillespie is of public school background and sounds it. The breeding comes through in his voice but, while one might accurately guess at Tonbridge, one would not immediately detect the inbuilt wit and humour of the man which makes him something a shade special in a world where many with similar educational upbringing hold the sort of stuffily conservative views which might be protective to their sport but are also undeniably restrictive. Edward Gillespie's politics are irrelevant and unknown to me, but nothing he does in his job at Cheltenham could be called overly conservative. His brain works in a way which blends commercial ideas into traditional frameworks. No doubt he has upset someone occasionally, but I would imagine the event has been rare. He has the happy knack of sitting comfortably on both sides of the fence and has achieved relative marvels in his three years in office. Tongue-in-cheek, he puts it down to the invaluable experience he gained while secretary of the Turf Club at York University. 'I arranged trips to racecourses and we had the odd meeting and function,' he says. 'But in truth, we didn't do much else. It did develop my interest in the sport, however, and I worked for United Racecourses – Sandown, Kempton and Epsom – before applying for the vacancy here at Cheltenham.'

The moment of reminiscing was interrupted by a large parcel entering the room, followed by a breathless man clutching it. It was the trophies for the Mackeson, and as they were anxiously checked through, someone told the type of funny story which seems forever to be at the elbow of racing folk. It was of a previous big race at Cheltenham, when the recipient of the major prize was Fred Winter. The trophy was a sculpture of a jockey on horseback and it had a short life. Minutes later part of it was picked up off the floor outside the weighing-room by a concerned bystander who, seeing the oblivious Mr Winter disappearing with the new central attraction of his mantelpiece, shouted after him: 'Fred, I've just found your head on the floor.'

A pair of Rolls-Royces sat elegantly outside the doors of the Queens Hotel, like swans in a duckpond. Night had fallen over the Imperial Gardens and when the sun came up again it would be Mackeson Gold Cup day. Friday's racing had been no better and no worse than the course management team had estimated and, although only thirty-four entered horses had stood their ground for the next day's card, ten of these were in the Mackeson, and it promised to be competitive. Now the long-distance reacegoers had retired to their hotels and boarding-houses, emerging by night to the eating-places and watering-holes of Regency Cheltenham. Nowhere, in this category, was better known as a punters' meeting-place than the Queens. For years now, it has been the gathering place of the Irish at Festival time, but for the rest of the year it retains, in the words of Egon Ronay, 'a feeling of opulence in the elegant foyer and the grand lounge'.

Inside the swing doors, calm prevailed. The hotel was not full, and shimmering staff ensured that life in this lavish oasis was kept on a smooth, untroubled course for its well-heeled patrons. Expensive, antique prints lined the walls, tasteful furniture decorated the public rooms and, in the main bar, four enormous potted palms provided more secluded corners than one would have thought possible in a high-ceilinged, square room.

The drinkers were, in the main, dressed for dinner and sipping cocktails. P.G. Wodehouse characters abounded, many no doubt down from

London for a weekend in the country. There was, I noticed, a conspicuous absence of racing chat and, in the time it took to down two glasses of expensive foreign lager, I did not hear one tip for the Mackeson meeting. On my way out, I satisfied idle interest by asking for the hotel's room tariff. It was £38 per person per night. I asked the receptionist to check the unlikely possibility that they may not yet be fully booked for the race Festival week. She looked at me blankly. 'Which week is that, sir?' I tottered out, skirted the sparkling Rolls-Royces and began to believe all the stories linking the Queens with racing had been a figment of imagination. Four months later I was to find out they were not.

Mist hung over Prestbury until well past breakfast-time on Saturday morning. There seemed no danger of it developing into the type of thick fog which has forced the abandonment of winter meetings in years gone by, neither did there seem any risk of rain. This was good news for Philip Arkwright, who had been casting anxious eyes at the grey sky since he arrived at the course from his Oxfordshire home around 7.30 am. Rain would have been ecstatically welcomed a few days earlier, but now it would only serve to make the firm ground as dangerous to horses as an ice-rink and quite possibly persuade a few more trainers against taking unnecessary early-season risks with their valuable animals. Clear, dry, and warm enough to attract crowds, was the weather-wish of Major Arkwright.

If the morning of such a major meeting could be likened to a military operation, Cheltenham had the man for the job. Philip had served the Army in Aden and Malaya, not to mention spells in Germany and Tidworth. He managed to indulge his love of riding during his career as a soldier and, when he came out of the army, he continued to ride both under rules and in point-to-points. Probably his best horse was Another, a moderate hurdler turned successful hunter-chaser under the training of Tim Forster. But when Philip stopped riding competitively, in 1974, he stopped riding completely, and in the decade since he has not so much as sat on a horse. He has, however, seen as many as most in his line of duty, first with the Warwickshire point-to-point and now as clerk at both Cheltenham and Haydock.

He shares more than just an office with Edward Gillespie. Both men have such pride in their work that sleep often refuses to come the night before a meeting. This may partly explain why both men were on site that Saturday morning at an hour when most Cheltenham residents were opening bleary eyes and wondering if they were suffering from the previous night, and many more had not reached that stage. Edward explains: 'Philip and I feel we have to be here in case of calamities, but as neither of us can sleep we might as well come in early, anyway.'

They were not lonely in their work. The maintenance men were in early, too, checking off minor, unseen but essential chores like the siting of advertisers' hoardings, the preparation of name boards and placement of direction signs. Catering delivery vans jostled for positions on the concourse and the shutters began to go up on the private catering franchises, like the seafood stand beloved of so many, and the doughnut stall which began selling its delightfully sticky wares at an almost obscenely early hour.

Doormen gathered in the warmth of the press room, sipping coffee away from the chill nip of the November wind and haggling over the relative quality of the tips they had garnered from trainers and other acquaintances. Outside again, at the top end of the course where the afternoon's participants had begun to settle in their boxes, stable-lads pattered about their business, every one with private dreams of leading his or her horse into the winners' enclosure within a few hours.

The course was like an awakening giant, but a few of the limbs slept blithely on. Down in the Tattersalls ring, where the great majority of heavy betting would be conducted during the afternoon, the bookies' stands had been left overnight – a jumble of wooden crates which resembled some crazy playground game.

By midday, things were buzzing. The bookmakers had arrived, forming an orderly queue to pay for their badges, permits to operate on the course. The jellied eels were selling well outside, the smoked salmon was popular in the members' stand and the *Sporting Life* seller, who had sat motionless and zombie-like on the steps to the entrance when I arrived, had leapt into comparatively frenzied action, distributing the 'punters' friend' papers with an accompaniment of unintelligible shouts.

The crowd was growing encouragingly, the atmosphere was good. Unfortunately, the day's racing began with the kind of farce that even the most scrupulous planners are powerless to avoid. Only three runners lined up for a £3000 qualifier in the Embassy Premier Chase series, which was disappointing enough. Worse still was the shape of the race, with the odds-on favourite, The Floorlayer, leading throughout and finishing alone, his two opponents having dumped their jockeys at different stages of the contest. One rider lay prone for some time and was clearly not at his best, but the other, sharply aware of the £599 prize money for the owner of the second-placed animal, rose from the deck and proceeded to pursue his playful horse, the inappropriately named Sweet Mandy, for fully five minutes before remounting and completing the course. It all caused plenty of chuckles but it was hardly the type of race Cheltenham strives to present.

Thankfully, the big race lived up to its billing, despite the late withdrawal of the extraordinary Grey Dolphin, who had already registered eight victories in the young season. Betting was confusingly open between the remaining nine runners, Fred Winter's Fifty Dollars More starting narrow favourite to win the race for the second successive year while Direct Line, from Yorkshire, had come in for heavy support and was, in the eyes of various sound judges, the pick of the paddock. Neither horse, however, figured in a compelling finish which saw local jockey Peter Scudamore, so often the bridesmaid and so seldom the bride on his own home course, touched off by a neck in a desperate battle between his mount, St Alezan, and Pounentes.

It was now that the essential spirit which pervades a major occasion at Cheltenham showed itself to triumphant effect. Pounentes was trained by an amiable Scotsman named Billy McGhie in a remote town called Lochmaben. Mr McGhie had only two horses in training and, of these, Pounentes was so far the only one to run. This was his fifth, and by far

The presentation line-up after Pounentes' victory in the 1983 Mackeson Gold Cup.

biggest win of the season and as he recovered himself from the splendid ovation which had greeted his horse from the banked and packed terracing of the winners' enclosure, beaming Billy told the assembled press: 'We've got two hundred and eighty miles to travel home and we'll be leaving in an hour. But I don't mind the journey one bit – we'll be travelling on air.'

The biggest trainers and the smallest win at Cheltenham. There are no barriers of class or status and every big win has its degree of romance; some, like Pounentes and Billy McGhie, have more than others.

Cheltenham staged the Champion Jockey's Ball that night, in honour of John Francome. By way of thanks from the chief guest, they received a little more than had been bargained for. The wounded champion, out for three weeks with an injury but now about to resume the quest for his fifth title, had not wasted the free time. At least, if his speech was not rehearsed, it was a masterpiece of bold spontaneous comedy which first bemused and then convulsed the various lords and ladies with whom he was sharing the top table. Seldom, if ever, can a mixed, dress dinner party have been treated to blue jokes made to sound so inoffensively hilarious. Francome at one stage climbed on top of the table to illustrate an especially dubious tale, and when he jumped down again it was to the sort of ovation he normally only receives for a particularly popular winner.

Francome, the son of a Swindon builder, has made himself rich by mixing devotion to hard work with displays of natural talent, and made himself a public favourite through his personality. He may be the best-known face National Hunt racing has ever boasted; certainly, no-one has matched him since the days of a dinner guest who laughed as loudly as anyone at his startling speech, Terry Biddlecombe.

Perhaps Biddlecombe's memory was rapidly flashing back seventeen years, to the night he stood before a similarly exalted audience as champion jockey. Again, the dinner was held at Cheltenham, though at the Queens Hotel rather than the racecourse. Again, it was in Mackeson week, though perhaps unwisely on the Friday rather than Saturday evening. Again, when the champion stood up to speak, he tried to be funny, though the lovable Biddles himself would admit that the response to his efforts was as distant as could be imagined from that afforded to his friend J. Francome.

It might all have been different for Biddlecombe if he had not broken his wrist. Forced to rest and miss the Mackeson meeting, he recalls drowning his sorrows in the cellar bar under the old Cheltenham stand during the Friday programme and being discovered after racing by his great friend and current houseguest, Josh Gifford, sleeping off his excesses in bed.

He recalls: 'Josh shook me frantically to wake me, saying: "You've got a speech to get ready for the dinner tonight." I was horrified – I had forgotten all about it.'

The two great jockeys together scribbled down a few notes. They knew Terry was due to be presented with a pair of prints for winning the jockeys' championship in 1965–66 and Josh jokingly said: 'Just thank everyone and leave it at that, because you are daft enough to say they would look lovely hanging in the cowshed!'

Biddlecombe, unfortunately, found the Gifford witticism too good to waste. He relates: 'I sat through dinner, trying to collect my thoughts. I had just managed to clear my head by the time the presentation was made ... I still thought the addition to my speech dreamt up by Josh was very witty and when my turn came to reply I stood up and said: "My lords, gentlemen, thank you very much for these two lovely Snaffles prints, which I am sure will look splendid hanging up in the cowshed," and paused, waiting for the laughter. There was a dreadful silence, broken only by a loud guffaw from Josh, somewhere in the sea of faces. It was terrible. I was so embarrassed it was not true. I managed to fluff my way through the remainder of my speech and sat down thankfully. I will never forget it. It was rude and stupid of me to say such a thing. I can only say that everybody there made nothing of it afterwards, and we had a terrific evening.'

Unlike the effervescent Francome, Biddlecombe is no natural comic, and it is quite inconceivable that he would have intended any insult to the Cheltenham course on which he doted throughout his riding days, and which he still loves to this day. Ask him for his favourite memory and a huge grin spreads across his face before he names, with absolute certainty, his 1967 Gold Cup triumph on Woodland Venture, a horse even trainer Fred Rimell had considered little better than a point-to-pointer.

Terry, a shade reluctant to gloat on past successes, explains: 'When I rode Gay Trip in the National and got beat a couple of lengths by Graham Thorner on Well To Do, I walked back in the weighing-room and there was Graham crying his eyes out. I thought "Jesus, it should be me crying, not him". But when I won the Gold Cup there were tears in my eyes too. It was a warm, unforgettable occasion.'

'We played cards and drank champagne all night and in the early morning I realised I would not physically be able to ride that day. I was due to go to Lingfield for Ron Smyth and had to lose 10 lb to do the weight. It meant sweating, taking pills and then driving a long way. Apart from that, I felt rough, so Josh phoned up and made an excuse for me.'

The '67 Gold Cup might just have crept into conversation during the lull before the Francome storm at dinner that night, for opposite Biddlecombe on his table in the racecourse Banqueting Suite was Stan Mellor, who had ridden the second horse, Stalbridge Colonist, in a memorable finish to the great race. Biddlecombe still recalls his thoughts as Mellor and his grey mount loomed up on his outside, going to the last fence. 'It put the fear of God in me because Stan was the last man I ever wanted to see taking me on in any race, let alone the Gold Cup – he was so good from the last fence.'

'On the run-in, Stan headed me for a few strides. I remember thinking "He's going to beat me," then "He has beaten me," when, within a stride, Woodland Venture was fighting back at him and I thought fiercely, "No way is he going to beat me!" I think that is the longest run-in I have ever experienced. I could hear Stan shouting but Woodland Venture lengthened his stride – and suddenly I had held him, to win. That feeling in the last few strides was so intense I will always remember it.'

The romance of the little man at Cheltenham was present that day, too. Woodland Venture had been bred and owned by a small-time Somerset farmer named Harry Collins, who was so keen to put a decent bet on his horse that, unknown to his disapproving wife, he took an old, barren cow to sell at his local market and raised an extra £100. As the horse started at 100–8 he had good reason to be pleased.

Biddlecombe was born in Gloucester and has never lived far from Cheltenham. His love affair with the great course began at an early age and, although Fred Winter rode ten more winners there than the Biddlecombe total of fifty-seven, his local associations mean that he remains the most popular of racing figures at Prestbury and, deep down, feels pangs of regret every time he watches, rather than rides in a race there. 'Riding at Cheltenham is something special – different from riding anywhere else,' he has often said.

He was once asked to describe in detail his movements and thoughts during a Cheltenham race day. It would begin, predictably enough, with a start at 6 am, riding out and maybe some schooling. Then, after a cup of coffee, he set off for the Turkish baths in his native Gloucester and sat there reading the *Sporting Life* and, if it was a big-race day and the adrenalin was flowing, sipping a glass or two of champagne.

He would walk the course, seeking out the best ground, checking the position of any marker dolls but also 'enjoying looking at those immaculate fences and hurdles'. Change, weigh out, walk to the parade ring, mount and set off towards the course again, this time with equine partner. 'The feeling as you turn out onto the track must be similar to that of coming out of the tunnel at Wembley – simply thrilling.'

Any butterflies, he says, have disappeared by the time you begin to circle at the start, brain totally tuned to the challenge. 'Cheltenham is

In the weighing room John Francome and Frank Berry and (below)
Geraldine Rees.

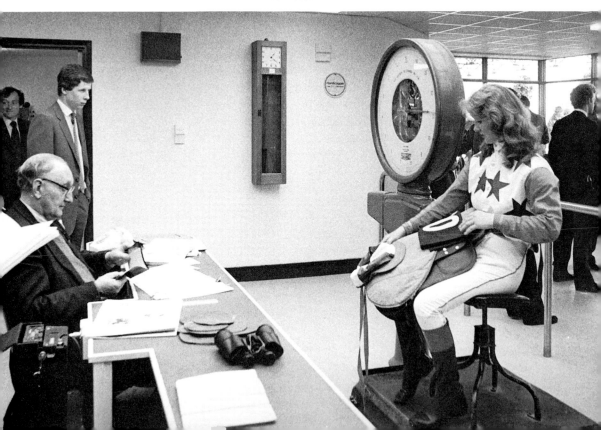

more demanding than any other track and if your horse runs away early on, you can forget about winning. Get him balanced as you get near the first, pick the place you're going to jump and hope everyone goes straight.'

Biddlecombe reckons that by the eighth fence in a Cheltenham chase, the race is sorting itself out. 'The bad ones are beginning to struggle and the good ones are emerging into challenging positions. As you turn towards the ditch at the far side, you can always see the dangers.' He used to try and steal a few lengths with a big jump at the ditch, then give his horse a second wind until breasting the top of the hill. 'If you're still on the bridle, you've got a chance – but if you're off the bridle, the prospect of those downhill fences is a little alarming. Inevitably, the pace increases. The next fence always seems bigger than all the others and you just hope you meet it right. A mistake here usually exacts its penalty. After this fence I used to let them run into the one in the dip and if I jumped it well and landed running I knew it would take a good one to beat me.

'At the final turn I never used to look round. Suddenly, that special Cheltenham feeling returns – there it is, the last fence. If it's met right and your horse picks up when you ask him, perhaps the thrill of victory really will be yours. Even then, the run-in can be a desperately long haul.'

Terry Biddlecombe won the Mackeson twice on Gay Trip, in 1969 and 1971. These were just two of his great memories of the course where, along with brother Tony, he used to sneak in over the wire fence by the water jump – two young boys starry-eyed at a spectacle that was to hook them both. Terry admits that every time he reached the farthest point of the course, by Frenchie Nicholson's old yard, he used to look across at the crowded stands and feel a touch of emotion. Probably it was nothing, though, to the emotion which almost drowned him on 14 March 1974 when he rode his last race – fittingly, if not inevitably, at Cheltenham. He had finished third in the Gold Cup aboard the Queen Mother's Game Spirit, nowhere in the County Hurdle on Bumble Boy. His final ride was on Amarind in the Cathcart Chase, the last event of the Festival and very often missed by thousands of the crowd, eager to beat the car park crush.

Very few left early, that year. Biddlecombe reluctantly led the parade, only after his fellow jockeys had insisted, and he confesses to being stunned as he came onto the course in front of the stands. 'I had no idea that so many would stay to watch my last race. The cheering was deafening and I couldn't believe it. Why on earth should anyone care that Terry Biddlecombe was retiring from racing?' But thousands did. Thousands remembered the winners he had ridden in inimitable style and many more cherished the character who was about to become such a severe loss to the sport. Some probably even remembered holding their breath as this apparently indestructible man had suffered some of the punishing falls that his loyal fans still speak of now. For Biddlecombe, the moment was almost too much.

'I do not think I have ever been so aware of the irresistible fascination Cheltenham has always held for me. It has caught me in its spell – seen my greatest triumph and many of my worst disasters. I knew then that I would never be free of its magnetism, nor ever wish to be as long as I drew breath.'

There was a party for Biddlecombe that night. As a rule, he enjoys parties. But this time he was too full with emotion, too reflective and regretful to even fancy a drink. He had one or two, of course, just to be sociable, but the overwhelming thought in his head was that he would never again ride at the course he loved so much.

He has never left it, however. The name T.W. Biddlecombe may not appear on the number boards these days but the ghost of Biddlecombe the rider still stalks the weighing-room and the cellar bar in the shape of stories recounted by the next generation of his antics and feats, and the man himself still stalks the course – a little heavier, a little older but no less fascinated by Prestbury. He lives ten miles from the course in the village of Corse Lawn, dreams of training horses and one day returning to the Cheltenham winners' enclosure. I wonder, however, whether it would feel the same, second time around or whether the legend of Terry the jockey should remain untouched. He remains truly one of Cheltenham's greatest heroes.

Chapter 5

ROME WAS NOT BUILT in a day, a racehorse does not become a champion overnight and no major sporting event is staged without many months of preparation. It does not take a super intelligence to realise that Cheltenham's annual festival, the meeting which brings together the champions of old and pits them against the champions of the future, is not thrown together over a few scrawled notes on the back of an envelope and a loud discussion over a bottle of bubbly. But precious few people outside the inner confines of the Steeplechase Company are aware quite how much time it all takes, quite how many headaches are suffered and barriers overcome before the tapes go up around two o'clock on the critical Tuesday afternoon in March.

Edward Gillespie explains the hard truth: 'By the time the Festival starts each March, we are already well underway with our planning for the next one.'

The bandwagon rolls slowly at first. Prices have to be fixed, for all enclosures, boxes and chalets; any alterations to race conditions and values confirmed; sponsorships negotiated. But during the summer months, when the racecourse is used for such unlikely events as dog-shows and circuses, administrative planning for the next great meeting is pushed ahead, advertising material prepared and an astonishing flood of enquiries dealt with.

By October of 1983, the seventy-three chalets planned for the Festival's tented village six months later, had all been sold, despite the fact that, at around £1,200 for the three-day meeting, they were twice as expensive as they had been two years earlier. 'We are rejigging to try and get more chalets in the space,' reported manager Gillespie, 'but the demand has been very encouraging. It is all a matter of convincing people that racing is not all about standing miserably in wellington boots in the mud of an overcrowded marquee. It can be done in comfort and style, and we have found that captains of industry will pay quite appreciable sums of money if they believe they can entertain their clients here in the proper manner.'

Steeplechasing, however, can never quite guarantee style and comfort ... even at Cheltenham. The New Year meeting of 1984 was blighted by some of the worst racing weather imaginable and, for those who did

Racecourse of the Year 1982. Tony Fairbairn, chairman of the Racegoers'
Club, *presents the award to Capt. Miles Gosling (left),* chairman of the
Steeplechase Co. Ltd.

brave the elements, there was a good deal of miserable standing around
in the mud, the wind and the rain. This meeting is traditionally the one
which brings people flocking for one of two reasons: they either want
some bracing air to rid their head of the New Year's Eve hangover; or
they want to prolong the festivities even further. The racing also happens
to be high class.

As New Year's Day fell on a Sunday, extending the country's Christmas break still further, Cheltenham's two-day programme was held on
the Monday and Tuesday. Monday's weather was tolerable – merely very
cold and windy. Tuesday was much worse. On the hills above Broadway,
only a dozen miles from the course, snow was falling heavily in mid-
morning, swept into car windscreens by a fierce gale which had howled
unabated all night, bringing down trees all around the area. Many potential racegoers doubtless turned back at this point, convinced that the

meeting would be abandoned and hastening with some relief back to their firesides. But the course itself had escaped the snow, and Philip Arkwright, in flat cap and wellingtons, topped off by thick waterproof coat, pulled a face as he returned to the weighing-room after a tramp on the windswept course. 'I almost wish I could find a reason to call it off,' he said, 'because we're not going to get any sort of crowd. But the course is perfectly raceable.'

Even Phil Hatcher's genial features were creased. He had woken at 5am, listened to the wind battering against the windows of his bungalow on the edge of the course and, against all his instincts, had wished he worked on a flat-racing course where his early-morning alarm calls would be confined to summer months and balmier weather. 'I walked round the course in the dark looking for gale damage, paddling in the wet patches which had formed. Some of the fences had been disturbed but it could have been a lot worse, and we were able to patch things up without many problems.'

Flurries of snow signalled the start of the meeting at noon but, re-markably, the sun broke through half-an-hour later as if in protest that the surprisingly large number of punters should have to suffer such dis-comforts. There was another Cheltenham romance, too, with the second race – a handicap hurdle named after Bryan Robinson's father Ernest – being won by Mossmorran, trained at Alnwick in Northumberland and owned by a group of Scottish milkmen who had all completed their rounds at dead of night in order to be on the road down to Cheltenham. They were boisterously triumphant in the unsaddling enclosure, and who could blame them?

The milkmen promised they would be back in ten weeks time for the Festival, and suddenly it did not seem such a distant threat after all. During that ten-week period, the tension would build around every mem-ber of the Cheltenham staff, and they would not have many days free of worries or hazards. The foot was now down on the accelerator pedal and preparations for the greatest racing show on earth were fully mobil-ised.

Every year, towards the end of January, a planning meeting is held at the course, where all involved bodies are expected to be represented so that everyone knows what everyone else is doing and areas of respon-sibility are clearly marked. The meeting is chaired by Captain Miles Gosling, chairman of the Steeplechase Company, and is highly civilised, preceded by coffee and followed by lunch. It was held this season on Thursday 19 January with the weather outside so crisp and perfect that every one of the twenty-two people gathered around a table in the press room wished they had come to watch racing and not talk business. All

Miss Caroline Beasley was the first lady rider to win at a Festival meeting when she won the 1983 Christie's Foxhunter Challenge Cup on Eliogarty.

twenty-two would be back again for the three-day meeting in March but the nature of their duties dictated that very few of them would see any racing at all.

The agenda was divided under six main headings: trains, coaches, police, car parks, security, staffing. Each had at least one spokesman but there was a suspicion of intimidating police presence in the line of seven uniformed officers down one side of the table, comprising two superintendents, three chief inspectors and two inspectors. British Rail had sent along four men, all in typically conservative suits, while Pratts, in charge of staffing, had three present, National Car Parks two and the Bristol Omnibus Company only one. At the far end of the table from the chairman sat Peter French from Racecourse Security Services – smart and assured, but chainsmoking. Another incessant smoker was Phil Hatcher, whose tweed jacket and tie were unconventionally set off by his habitual uniform, a pair of wellingtons.

In the two hours necessary to negotiate the agenda, the extent of the backstage operation unfolded. Some of the measures discussed, such as stewarding of the car parks and policing the royal visitors, were predictable and self-explanatory, but much of the business was of such detail that those thousands who arrive each year an hour before the first race and leave an hour after the last without a backward glance, would never dream that the racecourse officials involved themselves so intricately.

Take the trains. British Rail's representatives were asked for the number of special trains laid on from London (two on Tuesday and Wednesday, five on Thursday), for the cost of a champagne breakfast (£10.25) on any day and of the breakfast and dinner ticket (£20.50) on Thursday, and even for the dinner menu (steak, mushroom and oyster pie). There was also generous discussion about the routing and timings of the Orient Express, that lavish extravaganza normally peopled by foreigners with money to burn and journalists, on fat expense accounts, with stories to write.

Cheltenham's station staff are well accustomed to dealing with grumpy punters, inebriated punters and ticketless punters and the final train on Thursday, leaving at 7.30pm, has become known as 'The Sweeper', for its literal function in sweeping the remains of the day's crowd back to London.

There was a link between the trains and the buses, because the racecourse confirmed that they would continue to pay the bus company to take people from the course to the station without a ticket, in order to help the clearing of the car park after racing. At least two hundred coaches were expected on Gold Cup day and one major company had already intimated they would be bringing twenty-five per cent more than the previous year. The man in charge of car parking scratched his head and grimaced at the prospect.

If all this business had begun to sound menially monotonous, there was more to come. The police, to my great surprise, were well aware of

George Excell, senior fence builder.

the average racegoer's anger when he is held up by what look suspiciously like non-essential roadworks on the most popular route to a major meeting. Furthermore, they had undertaken to write to the Public Works' department asking them to refrain from such practices unless absolutely necessary. Never again will I curse the police when sitting fuming in a two-mile tail-back just outside Cheltenham.

Anyone who has battled unsuccessfully to get a taxi into or out of the course may care to know that only ninety-nine permits are issued by police enabling drivers to enter the racecourse. And all those who have driven around for what seemed like hours, in growing irritation at the lack of street parking in the area of the course, will be fascinated at the knowledge that the police use more than four hundred no parking signs in the immediate vicinity.

Traffic is but one of the police's functions at the Festival, however, and by no means the most important when seen in the light of law and order enforcement. On criminal matters, they work in close collaboration with racing's private 'police force', Racecourse Security Services, and neither seems jealous of the other's authority.

71

One of their major problems is presented by pickpockets. Just as flowers come out when the sun shines, so pickpockets will appear wherever there is a guaranteed crowd and, for all the precautionary measures the police can produce and all the warnings the course can issue, some undoubtedly flourish every year at Cheltenham. Maybe some of the warnings have not been ideally worded. As Edward Gillespie related with great amusement: 'One public address announcement last year stated, "Ladies and gentlemen, may we advise you there are pickpockets operating on the course today." It made it sound as if we had gone to great expense to get them here!'

Someone else pointed out that two posters had also become embarrassingly muddled on a wall of the stand so that they read: 'Bet with the Tote and beware of pickpockets.'

The subject was not taken lightly, however, and the police reported that a new surveillance camera would probably be sited on top of the jockeys' number board, aimed at the narrow transfer channels between the members' enclosure and the bookmakers, a favourite hunting ground for the pickpocketing fraternity. 'They work in teams,' explained Peter French. 'One will push the victim, apologise and pick his pocket, then swiftly pass on the wallet or purse to his accomplice, who will be away through the crowd before anyone realises what has happened.' Extra police officers were to be brought in from Liverpool to counter, and hopefully recognise, the expected influx of light-fingered thieves from their own area.

Bomb scares provided another delicate subject but, as there were no CID men in the seven-strong police team present, no-one was qualified to answer the course officials' questions. All that could be resolved was that Miles Gosling would be issued with a bleeper so that he could be contacted anywhere on the course in the event of such an alert. A swift decision would then be taken on whether the course should be cleared. The matter of how it would be cleared was to be discussed later, with CID assistance.

Plain-clothes detectives attend the Festival meeting in substantial numbers but their anonymity had been threatened, the previous year, by the siting of their caravan base in an area clearly visible to most of the crowd. Anyone planning a criminal operation had only to watch the caravan for half-an-hour to identify every plain-clothes man on the course. It was to be different this year.

The police were to be operational on the course by eight o'clock each morning but one of their off-course duties was the annual Thursday morning royal visit to Prestbury village, at which the Queen Mother, en route for Badminton, diverts to buy sweets at a grocer she has patronised for many years. The police, understandably, treated the extra burden

Bregawn (Graham Bradley) clears the last fence in the 1983 Gold Cup to win from Captain John (left). The first five horses were all trained by Michael Dickinson – a feat unlikely ever to be repeated.

with more resignation than enthusiasm, for nothing was more certain than that the villagers would flock into the streets in their hundreds to catch a glimpse, maybe even a word, with racing's favourite lady.

Racecourse Security Services, as the name implies, confine their efforts to activities occurring on the course. They are empowered to investigate suspected frauds by owners or trainers and suspected fiddles by jockeys, but their more regular routine involves the settlement of disputes between punters and bookmakers and the enforcement of security at the gates.

At the 1983 Festival, they dealt with one hundred and fifty two disputes in the betting ring, which was a slight reduction on the previous year's figure. For 1984, they planned to have six ring inspectors in Tattersalls and three in the Silver Ring (the cheap enclosure in the centre of the course). 'We have to be discreet,' says Peter French, 'and there are times when the bookies are unco-operative and then there is nothing we can do.'

The security men keep a watchful eye open for radios used by bookies' scouts as a link with their bosses; these are prohibited on any racecourse. They may also eject anyone caught extorting money from punters for tips, most of which – in my experience – are fanciful, anyway. They are not so concerned with characters like the gentleman who, apparently, sells racecards in the car park all afternoon and then, as the crowds begin to leave, dons dark glasses, an old mackintosh and a faraway look to play a mouth organ at the gate, cap placed at the ready for collection of unwanted coins. Such men as these are not only harmless, but the stuff of racecourse folklore, and, as such, not to be tampered with.

Illegal entry into the course falls somewhere in the grey area between police and security. Everyone knows it happens, and with such an enormous choice of possible points of entry, there is a limit to what can be done about it. Most local jockeys and trainers freely admit that, in their own childhood, they frequently slipped into the course through a hedge or over a fence and, as Peter French confesses: 'We can't waste too much time trying to catch one fellow who hasn't paid, because we would probably miss twelve more.'

A similar, phlegmatic attitude is adopted to the time-honoured means of securing a prime car parking place by slipping the steward a £5 note through the window. No-one knows how much 'bonus money' the parking attendants pick up during Festival week and no-one is in any great rush to find out. Only if the practice spawned open warfare between queuing motorists would the police consider it their business to interfere.

Forging tickets is altogether different, and one of the most severe headaches encountered by the security services. Three years ago, a large number of members' badges were discovered to be very clever fakes, mostly in the possession of unwitting innocents who had handed over money in good faith to their unscrupulous ticket tout. RSS was determined such a large-scale fraud would not occur again and, with much help from the Steeplechase Company, the design of badges and the procedure for distribution was altered. Different-coloured threads were now woven into the cord on each badge, making them virtually impossible to copy, and none were sent out until four weeks before the meeting to further reduce the time available to any persistent would-be forger.

Peter French's team, however, were not about to start kidding themselves that the criminal element had been obliterated by such measures. There was to be no complacency. 'I will have men standing alongside the gatemen, and they are there to check the badges and, it must be said, to check on the gatemen. No-one is to be allowed in without paying and gatemen have been known to accept bribes or let in their mates in the past. Our job is to make sure there is as little fiddling on this course as possible, but to do it in such a manner that we are not conspicuous to the general public who have paid money to enjoy themselves.' Mr French, who would have a staff of ten working with him during the Festival meeting, took out yet another cigarette and lit up while the police discussed the previous year's regrettable incident in which a member of the public had slipped through their defences, gained entry to the unsaddling enclosure and, much worse, approached and shaken the hand of the Queen Mother. He had then escaped, probably intending to do no more and perhaps not considering himself any kind of security risk. But the police had to view him as such, and they would be especially on the lookout for him this year. With around two hundred uniformed bobbies on duty, they meant to catch him, too.

The meeting returned to meniality with some heated debate over whether a turnstile should be erected on the new entrance next to the banqueting suite. It seemed a small point to arouse such feelings, but it perfectly illustrated the enthusiasm with which every possible defect is tested thoroughly before the meeting even begins.

Something would go wrong: it always does. But no-one could accuse these men of not trying to prevent it.

During the Festival meeting the parade of horses is led by huntsmen of local packs – a different hunt on each day. Here it is the turn of the Cotswold being led by the Master, Mr Tim Unwin.

Chapter 6

SOMETIMES, EVEN IN THE precarious world of National Hunt racing, things fall so perfectly into place that claims of divine intervention have to be taken seriously. This was the case when Ireland's greatest champion horse won his third and last Gold Cup - on St Patrick's Day, 1966. The loyal Irish had rightly been scornful of any suggestion that their darling Arkle could be beaten, pointing out for emphasis that St Patrick himself would not allow it. Only three horses dared to take on Arkle, who started at an absurd but predictable 10 to 1 on and won by thirty lengths, though not before making a cataclysmic mistake at the eleventh fence which would assuredly have floored any animal which did not have (a) the strength and athleticism of chasing's greatest hero, and (b) the support of a patron saint. On such incidents is the Irish faith built, and their love affair with Cheltenham nourished.

Arkle had worn a sprig of shamrock that day and, as he returned to the dewy-eyed cheering of his legion of fans, a plane flew over the racecourse and deposited about another half-a-ton of the stuff. The horse's countrymen had plainly not been lacking in confidence. Neither, to be sure, had his jockey, Pat Taaffe.

Almost two decades on, Taaffe walked with a more pronounced stoop and carried a head of greyer hair than his supporters of old would remember. At first glance, emerging from the shadows of the stable-boxes at his home in County Kildare, he looked to have aged unkindly for one who was not fifty-four until the eve of the 1984 Festival. But it was no more than an illusion. The mere mention of Arkle brought a sparkle to his eyes, took years off his features. I had come to ask him about the horse and he needed no great prompting.

'There will never be a horse to touch him,' he said with absolute certainty in his gently lilting voice. 'If they weren't going quick enough for him in a race, he would go on to make the pace himself ... and they would not catch him very often. He was intelligent, consistent. He knew exactly what he was going to do, and almost invariably, he did it.'

Arkle was a Cheltenham phenomenon. If any horse has ever been the subject of more passionate support at the Festival, I have not heard of him. He was entered for three Gold Cups and he won them all, in the process breaking the hearts of the connections of England's Mill House who, in any other era, would almost certainly have run up a sequence of Gold Cups himself. Mill House, trained by Fulke Walwyn, won the 1963 event when favourite but was then twice beaten – first by five lengths and then by twenty – by his great rival from 'across the water'. The duels were seen as nothing less than England against Ireland, winner take all. The great irony was that Mill House had been broken in by Pat Taaffe before being sent to England to be trained.

'I thought he would be a champion,' reflected Taaffe. 'After I had broken him and he had gone across to England, I wrote to Willie Robinson, who was riding for Mr Walwyn, and told him how good the horse was. Then six months later, when Arkle arrived on the scene, I wrote to him again and just said I thought we'd got one who was even better.'

When the horses first met, in the Hennessy Gold Cup at Newbury in November of 1963, the contest was won and lost at the third last fence, where Arkle slipped on landing. He recovered his balance and ran on gamely, but Mill House had flown. It was a brief glory for the English to savour, altogether a false dawn. For, as Taaffe promised to Arkle's owner, the Duchess of Westminster, Mill House never beat him again.

In the 1964 Gold Cup, Mill House started favourite, but the Irish, pouring into the Cotswolds laden with cash and puffed up with pride, would not hear of Arkle being defeated. Mill House was still three lengths up on the Irish challenger at the second last. But Taaffe, who had as usual received no specific instructions from the trainer Tom Dreaper, had taken the advice of fellow jockey Dave Dick and saved Arkle for a finishing burst. He was later to compare his tactics that day with those often employed by Steve Ovett – if you know you have a better finish than your rivals, get in a position to use it when it matters. Arkle accelerated clear. The legend was born.

He won the next two Gold Cups with disdainful ease. How many more he might have won is a question no-one can confidently answer, but Dreaper, Taaffe and everyone else in the know believed the horse to be still at his peak when he went to Kempton Park in December of 1966 to try and win the prestigious King George VI Chase for a second successive year. In the field against him were Dormant, who had been second the previous season, and Woodland Venture, who was to win the Gold Cup for Terry Biddlecombe three months later. Both Biddlecombe and Jeff King, who rode Dormant, freely admit they would have stood no chance with Arkle at his best. But at some point in the race, Arkle hit a fence so hard that he cracked a pedal-bone. Gallant to the end, he kept going. King recalls: 'Woodland Venture fell at the second last and I was delighted at the thought of finishing second to Arkle. But as he approached the last ahead of me there was plainly something wrong. On

In 1982 Arkle's twenty-fifth birthday was celebrated with a champagne breakfast around his statue. Left to right *Major Philip Arkwright, Edward Gillespie and Lord Oaksey.*

the run-in he was only waddling compared to his normal gallop and we got up to win. But it was a sad way to do it.' Many thousands more were echoing King's sentiments that night as it became clear Arkle's future was in serious doubt.

There was widespread mourning in Ireland. Get-well cards were sent to the stricken horse's stable and dutifully pinned on the door by concerned staff. A security firm had to be called in to control the hordes of people who turned up at the yard, hoping for a glimpse of the horse, like visitors to a sick film-star in hospital. Horses were never meant to cause such public pandemonium.

But Arkle never did recover adequately, and was given an honourable retirement, having won more than £75,000 in prize money – quite a haul for a horse who was bought for just 1,150 guineas when a distinctly unattractive three-year-old.

Pat Taaffe was only ever to be reunited with his great equine friend at occasional charity appearances. He missed the horse, as he had every right to do, and when Arkle died, and was buried on the Duchess's land, it would not surprise me if his equally capable jockey shed a tear or two. Not that it was quite the end for Arkle. His body was later dug up and mounted for show at the National Stud Museum in Ireland. Pat went to the opening, and there was emotion in his eyes as he remembered the experience. 'I hated seeing his frame up there,' he said. 'I couldn't look at him for long.'

After Arkle's final Gold Cup in 1966, however, Taaffe had been absent from the winners' enclosure for only a year before Fort Leney brought him yet another triumph. Like Arkle, Fort Leney was trained in Ireland by Tom Dreaper and, if he was never quite in the incomparable class of his predecessor, he was very much a hero. For, after one show of temperament in the Scottish National a couple of years earlier, a full vet's examination had shown Fort Leney to have a hole in his heart. Six months of treatment and observation by a heart specialist restored the horse to racing fitness, the one medical proviso being that a jockey should not use a whip on him. But in March 1968, coming up the Cheltenham hill with the tenacious Jeff King upsides him on The Laird, Taaffe weighed up the advice, assessed the proven toughness of his horse and gave him a few cracks. Fort Leney battled on to win by half-a-length.

In all, Taaffe rode thirty-two winners at Cheltenham, which is still the highest number by any Irish-based rider. He retired from the saddle in 1970 but kept coming back to Cheltenham in his new role as a trainer. In 1974, he became only the third man to achieve the double of riding and training a Gold Cup winner when Captain Christy, at 7-1, beat Fulke Walwyn's The Dikler, the previous year's winner, by five lengths.

With fluctuating numbers of horses, and varying degrees of success, Taaffe continued training until 1982. But when he sits back now in the front-room of his high-ceilinged house in the remote backwoods of little Straffan, the photographs of his feats looking down from every wall, he does not sound as if he especially enjoyed it.

'Many people don't realise that the trainer's average day is about twice as long as the jockey's. But it is more than that. There is the worry, too. I never had much anxiety when I was riding. Even in Arkle's greatest days, I didn't worry about the horse and his well-being, only about my job in getting him round safely and winning. As a trainer it was very different – there were so many little things to make me anxious. I found that, in training, I didn't actually enjoy racing. I just got through it and then enjoyed looking back if I had had a winner.

'I suppose I eventually packed up because I became a bit disillusioned. Most people who want to own horses nowadays are only in it for the gambling. There are some notable exceptions, of course, but I found this to be the rule. If their horse wins, you are the best trainer in the world. If it doesn't, and there is no good exsuse, then someone is going to get the blame and it's very likely to be the trainer.

'It's not that I could not take criticism, or that I was scared of it, just

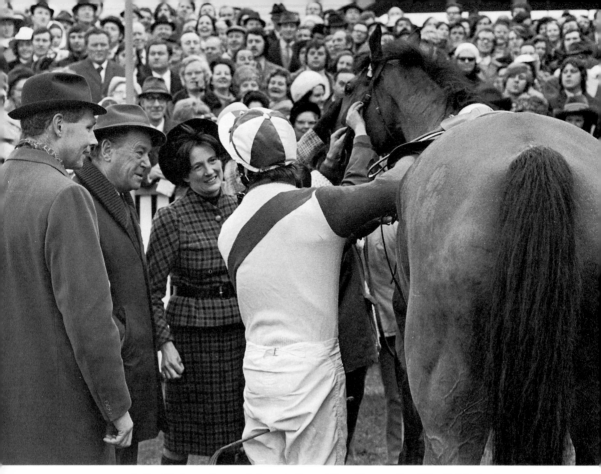

Fulke Walwyn (second from left) and Ron Barry after The Dikler's victory in the 1973 Gold Cup.

that I grew a little tired of constantly feeling under pressure to produce horses to win for the big bet. So I stopped. I still train a couple for myself, and I enjoy breaking in other people's horses. The yard is still here, and in good working order, and if my son Tom wants to take it over at any time, it's ready for him.'

Tom, having started his riding life as an amateur and forged a successful link with local trainer Arthur Moore, was now a thriving professional, looking forward to a clutch of attractive rides at the 1984 Cheltenham Festival. But Pat would be with him only in spirit. He no longer travelled much to watch racing, preferring to put his feet up with the television and the video, an essentially private man making his assessments and taking his pleasure alone, rather than in the throng of the racing folk with whom he mixed for so long.

'I haven't been to Cheltenham for three years. I miss the atmosphere, certainly, and I think if Tom gets a ride in the Gold Cup one year soon then I will go. But in general, you know, I'm quite happy watching racing on television here in my own home.'

No man who has had the association with Cheltenham that Pat Taaffe has had over the years can be entirely impervious to its magnetism, and he still plainly revels in his memories.

'I always used to go to the Champion Jockey's dinner the night before the Mackeson, and I must admit I never felt too good the next morning. But during the Festival I would try hard to look after myself a little better than that. I remember going to the Hunt Dance at Cirencester more than once, and it was all too easy to get swept up by the spirit of it all. You think you are going for one drink and then an early night, but before you know it you're three parts to the wind.

BBC commentator Peter O'Sullevan chatting to Tommy Carberry, one of the most successful Irish jockeys to have ridden at Cheltenham, during the early morning gallops on the course at the 1983 Festival.

'The Queens was a place to be avoided in Festival week and I never stopped there. Those who did were always getting involved in card games which went on through the night. I know men who gambled everything they'd got and more, before they even got to the races. It was a hopeless place during Cheltenham week. I always used to stay at The Carlton and tried not to get too involved in the festivities. It was a much quieter place – Peter O'Sullevan always stayed there, too – and to avoid the battle of car parking I would generally walk to the course. It took about fifteen minutes but it was good morning exercise, and fascinating with it.'

Pat and his wife Molly had five children. Two of them were boys and of these only Tom had tried to shadow the career of his famous father. So far he was not making a bad job of it at all. True, his first visit to Cheltenham, in 1982, had brought a fine and a severe rebuke for excessive use of the whip, but it had also brought him to prominence, persuaded him to turn professional and given quiet, meditative Pat real cause to think that, one day, he might be revisiting old Cotswold haunts, perhaps not just in the cause of seeing his son ride in the Gold Cup, but maybe even winning it.

Meantime, he had his memories. 'All of us in the weighing-room would have a few glasses of champagne after the Gold Cup. It was traditional – the bottles were sent in for us to share around. But some of the jockeys didn't confine themselves to that. I remember Terry Biddlecombe, for instance ... I used to marvel at how he rode so brilliantly, for so long, because I can recall him ordering up crates of champagne in the weighing-room between races, from that old cellar bar. He would offer it all round, but by the end of the day he would have had a few glasses himself. Out on the course, though, he was a great professional – all his joviality was forgotten and he just became the top rider he always was. I shall never forget him at Cheltenham ...'

A few miles further into the Kildare wilderness, along a pot-holed track apparently leading out the back door of civilisation, Tom Taaffe's trainer Arthur Moore was very much looking forward to Cheltenham. Indeed, he gave the distinct impression that it would need civil war between England and Ireland to make him miss it – and even then, he might consider defecting for the week.

At thirty-four years of age, Moore was one of the most consistently successful of Irish jump trainers. Also one of the most regular of raiders on the top English prizes during the jump season. The year of 1984 had already been kind to him, with his game hurdler Fredcoteri having won the valuable Irish Sweeps Handicap at Leopardstown for the second successive season, young T.J. Taaffe the visibly jubilant jockey. Now it was time to plan the most important campaign of all. Arthur Moore was well aware that, each time he goes to Cheltenham, he is not only representing himself and his owners, but representing Ireland against England. He relished the challenge.

His enthusiasm was not surprising in view of his breeding. Arthur's father was the late Dan Moore, who rode immediately after the war – finishing second in the 1947 Gold Cup aboard Dorothy Paget's Happy Home – and later turned triumphantly to training, producing L'Escargot to win the first two Gold Cups of the 70s in the brilliantly sympathetic hands of Tommy Carberry. But Dan Moore was also responsible for a horse who perhaps became still more popular, still more famous, for the tragic rather than the triumphant. His name was Tied Cottage.

In all, Tied Cottage ran five times in the Gold Cup and the record books claim he never won the race – second place to Davy Lad at his first attempt in 1977 being his best official effort. Statistics can lie, sometimes cruelly. Tied Cottage should have won the race twice – once, he lost it with a slip and a pitch after the final fence, another time he lost it weeks after he had actually gone past the post in first place.

It was in 1979 that he came to the last fractionally ahead of the Peter Easterby-trained Alverton, ridden by another of Ireland's favourite sons, Jonjo O'Neill. Snow was falling heavily, and whether it had added a fatally greasy top to the already heavy going, only Tied Cottage himself will know. The fact is he landed in front of Alverton and the Irish punters who had taken the 12-1 starting price were opening their lungs to roar him home up the hill when he came down. Alverton, who only weeks later was to break his neck and die in the Grand National, completed the course in comfort, totally unchallenged. Dan Moore thought of what might have been.

A year later, the name D.L. Moore actually appeared as the winning trainer in all the morning papers on 14 March. To all intents and purposes, Tied Cottage had won the Gold Cup. Starting at 13-2, surprisingly generous when one considers his run of twelve months earlier, Tommy Carberry's mount made all the running and came home eight lengths clear of Master Smudge. It may well have been a sub-standard Gold Cup – heavy rain the night before had brought the withdrawal of two fancied runners and the field was not strong enough to stand such defections. Nevertheless, Carberry had ridden a superb race, waiting in front, giving his horse breathers when it seemed to the uncommitted he was about to be swallowed up, and then accelerating away again. He was a worthy winner, and it was nothing short of a tragedy that the race was subsequently taken away from him on such a minor and, by the inquiry's admission, unavoidable technicality as the trace of theobromide which appeared in the horse's urine test.

Dan Moore, maybe broken-hearted at the disqualification on such

*Tied Cottage goes down in front of Alverton in the 1979 Gold Cup. Tragically
Alverton was to be killed a few weeks later in the Grand National.*

infuriating grounds of his bravest horse, died a few months later. Tragically, Tied Cottage's owner Anthony Robinson, who rode the horse to victory in the Irish National, also died within the year. Arthur Moore, who had been acting as assistant trainer since before L'Escargot's first Cheltenham win, took on full responsibility with heavy heart but total motivation. When, the following March, Drumgora carried the stable's colours to victory in the Queen Mother Champion Chase; the main event on day two of the Festival, A.L.T. Moore admits to understandable overdoing of the celebrations. 'It was,' he explains, 'my first training winner at Cheltenham, which would have been cause enough. But it was so close to the anxiety and disappointment we had all suffered over Tied Cottage, and then the death of father, that I think it rates as my most satisfying win anywhere, anytime.

'It sounds funny now, I suppose, but I had never really meant to train. I rented a yard on The Curragh at first but when I came here with my wife, Mary, we meant to develop it as a stud farm. The training happened virtually by accident.'

A happy accident. Since Dan's death, son Arthur has built the business on efficient, progressive lines. He now has around forty horses installed, mostly jumpers but flat horses good enough to win at the major English courses when they run. Schooling grounds and gallops are set up just across the road, on sixty acres of his own bogside land, and in his own, recently extended house, surrounded by an enviable collection of Snaffles prints, Arthur presents a contented picture. He has a wife, three children and no desire to move.

Moore was educated in England at Downside and he is often asked why he does not move back to expand his training business and exploit the greater financial opportunities on the east of the Irish sea. He shakes his head at every such suggestion. 'Our roots are settled in Ireland. We will never move now ... but it's nice to go across to England and win some of their prize money.'

He had done that often, and now he was scheming to do it again. Within the stable-yard he calls Dereens were housed some of Ireland's finest jumping horses, some of the animals on which punts would be plunged, come March. Arthur, who is the type to consider every question carefully and then give a thoroughly unemotional answer, was far too clever to begin bragging noisily about the Festival prospects of his charges, but there were traces of confidence as he discussed the meeting, and more than mere traces of enthusiasm.

He spoke of Drumgora, who would be aimed for the Champion Chase again, of The Brockshee, who won the Arkle Chase two years earlier and now had a choice of engagements, of Royal Bond who was pencilled in for another shot at the Gold Cup, and of Fredcoteri, who would take his chance in the Champion Hurdle. He spoke, too, of the horse he had trained and then lost – Venture to Cognac. Moore bought the horse for only £950 at Doncaster sales, ran him in bumper races (National Hunt flat races) in Ireland and then sold him to the Sherwood family. Oliver Sherwood had worked as assistant to Moore for three years before going back to England and joining Fred Winter. The horse went with him and became a live Gold Cup candidate. Sherwood and Moore remained close friends. Such is racing.

Like everyone else involved in Irish racing, Moore finds it hard not to get swept up and carried away by talk of Cheltenham, probably far too soon in the season. 'It is such a big thing to the Irish that every horse is channelled that way,' he explains. 'Some animal might win a moderate novice chase on a tin-pot course in November and immediately he is put down as a natural to win the Arkle Chase at the Festival. It's ridiculous, really, but it's no more than natural enthusiasm. I try to keep my feet on the ground, sort out which horses might be good enough from those which never will be, and give them the type of preparation I feel they need.'

Moore has inherited his father's love of the Festival and it showed through. 'We will have fun there, as we always do. We stay in a small hotel, outside the town and away from the real hub of the action. But there is a sociable group of us and we know how to enjoy ourselves. For me, the racing comes first and last. But Cheltenham would not be Cheltenham without a bit of fun.'

Dawn Run was the Irishman's Cheltenham banker long before March came around. Had she not given the reigning champion hurdler, Gaye Brief, a terrible fright at Liverpool the previous April, and a mere twenty-four hours after winning a valuable hurdle by a street? Did that not mean she was worth the maximum bet, the maximum excitement, as the great expedition came around again? Every Irish racing man, be he professional punter or priest, seemed to think so. Well, most of them.

In December the mare suffered a surprise defeat when beaten convincingly by Boreen Deas at Naas. Jonjo O'Neill, who had flown across from England for the ride, was not downcast. Indeed, he insisted: 'This was a top-class race and she gave a stone and a half to the winner, with the rest nowhere. Everyone is crabbing her, but I couldn't be more pleased.' With that, Jonjo hustled off for the night flight back to Newcastle, still wondering whether he would be offered the ride on the pride of Ireland in the one race that really mattered, the Champion Hurdle.

But one man was distinctly unimpressed. Leaning on a wooden rail in the dingy but atmospheric room at Naas which combines roles as weighing-room, press-room and tea-bar, he shook his head over the performance of the champion-elect and thought back to his own Cheltenham triumph of not so long ago.

Tommy Kinane looked every inch the Irish ex-jockey: small, slight, even a little gnarled of face. He had turned to training after winning the Champion Hurdle on Monksfield in 1978, surrounding himself with the plentiful racing members of the Kinane family and producing a good supply of winners. But Cheltenham, not surprisingly, still ranked as his favourite track. He had definite ideas on how the course should be ridden, positive views on the merits of the horses he had just seen. 'None of these will win the Champion Hurdle,' he said. 'Gaye Brief is no flier, mind, but he will win again – unless you English have got something else up your sleeves over there. We've got nothing in Ireland to beat him. Dawn Run is a good mare but she just lacks that bit of class.

'You have to ride Cheltenham a certain way – you can't hope to come from a long way back and win, it's not that sort of track. When I won on Monksfield I rode my own race, always up with the pace and going on when the time was right. I would have won the previous year, too, if I'd been allowed to ride the horse that way.'

Kinane, the little man whose broad grin lights up a giant colour picture looking down on a stairway in the new stand at Cheltenham, was quite certain in his own mind. Dawn Run would not win at the Festival. But then neither he, nor Jonjo O'Neill – nor anyone else for that matter – could have had any idea of the drama to come. The Irish just packed their bags, saved their money and hoped for the best. It was back in England that the story was taken up.

Chapter 7

JUST AS A PARTY is only really enjoyable if you don't have to stay behind and clear up the mess, so a great sporting event is much more attractive to those whose home town is not being invaded by the crowds. Cheltenham, a prosperous but peaceful place for fifty-one weeks of the year, puts on a gaudy, noisy disguise for a few days in March and it would be asking too much to expect every one of the eighty-six thousand residents to be pleased about it.

The architects who were commissioned to rebuild the thriving spa town in the early 1800s, injecting Greek influence on the traditional Cotswold stone of before, may well turn in their graves at news of the thousands who descend on their elegant creation each spring with only betting and boozing in mind. As the girl in the tourist office confirmed: 'They find Cheltenham a bit quiet. They ask us for casinos or gambling clubs, and there are none here. We get the odd enquiry about illegal activities, too . . .'

But the local lady, interviewed on the area's commercial radio station, Severn Sound, about the residents' reaction to Festival time, probably summed up the general feeling when she said: 'It's like Las Vegas for a week. Cheltenham comes to life. The people here wouldn't like it to happen every week but because it's only once a year, they enjoy it.'

There is something incongruous about it all, though. In a town where messrs Lear & Lear, Lawson & Lawson and other assorted estate agents think nothing of offering properties for sale at upwards of £200,000, where the shops are up-market and expensive, the restaurants lavish and the image persists of retired colonels in their bathchairs, thousands of prospective punters, many from motley, mundane backgrounds, make improbable visitors.

John Ryde, who works for one of Cheltenham's estate agents but is a passionate historian of the town and the racecourse, developed the theme, suggesting: 'There is a love-hate relationship between the racecourse and the town. Those who don't like racing tend to think racegoers are profligate, a little vulgar, and that they never look at the beauty of the town.'

Mr Ryde is one who considers the town should make much more capital of the fact that they have the world's most famous racecourse on the doorstep, encouraging and fostering links with the racing fraternity rather than – as happens in some cases – treating the existence of the course as something to be tolerated and, if possible, ignored. His views are shared by local photographer Bernard Parkin, who has seldom missed a racing day at Cheltenham since he first attended the Festival as a wartime schoolboy in 1941.

Bernard used to live within eyesight and earshot of the course and remembers, as a boy, watching the race fans stream past the family front door on their walk from the station to the races. 'Cheltenham was a great focal point of racing in those days,' he says, 'but that doesn't apply now. Every pub in Prestbury was full of racing chatter up to the early 60s – then the trainers based locally began to move out, or retire for various reasons, until now the racecourse itself is almost the only evidence that Cheltenham is a racing town.'

It is, however, impressive evidence, and in the week leading up to the Festival one would have to be a monk, or have a permanent job underground, to escape the knowledge of what was about to happen. The town abandons whatever prejudices it may have had and gears itself to making the most of the event. Business is bound to be good around the town and, for those in the hotel, catering or licensing trades, it will inevitably be the best week of the year.

Cheltenham literally bursts at the seams. Well provided though it is for hotel accommodation, with almost four hundred rooms in top-class hotels listed in Egon Ronay's guide plus a preponderance of cheaper boarding-houses, there is nowhere near sufficient to cope with the enormous influx. The accommodation agency in the town centre works at full stretch in the weeks leading up to the meeting, and spreads its tentacles far and wide. Many racegoers, especially those over from Ireland, are prepared to take a room thirty or even forty miles out of town, and the hotels in Stratford, Bristol and Swindon all profit from race business. Some, of course, profit more than others. Human nature appears to dictate that whenever a trader is guaranteed a glut of business, he will increase his prices. There is nothing anyone can do to prevent a hotelier charging just what he likes for his rooms in Cheltenham week, for he knows very well that there will always be people who have left it late to book and who are willing to grab at anything to make sure they have a bed to sleep on. The tourist office agrees that certain hotels charge 'extortionate' rates during Festival week, and my own efforts to find accommodation certainly uncovered some fanciful prices. Many places had devised all-in deals, the most expensive I found being the De La Bere, the splendid country house on the very edge of the course in Prestbury, which was asking £660 per double room for a four-night stay including meals. Just up the road on Cleeve Hill, the Malvern View – which boasts

The Queens Hotel, Cheltenham – a hive of activity during the Festival.

one of the finest restaurants for miles around but offers much more basic rooms than its neighbour – set its rate for a similar stay at £400. The Golden Valley, den of many Irishmen, charged a simple £72 per night per room, meals not included, and The Carlton, where Pat Taaffe always used to stay, was more modest still at £40 per night. If you wanted to be in amongst the action at the Queens, it would cost you £53 for a single room, including breakfast, and if you sought a more peaceful time at the excellent Wyastone in Montpelier, the price was £45 a night.

You could hardly get closer to the course than the Prestbury House Hotel, but neither could you get in. They reported that their rooms, at £27.83 per person per night, were booked by regular customers each year in advance, and sounded suitably scandalised at the suggestion that they just might have a cancellation.

Those who choose to travel fifteen miles a day and stay at Broadway, in the ornate and olde-worlde splendour of the Lygon Arms, would pay £166 a night for two people in a double room and not much less than that for a decent dinner. But there were plenty willing to dig deep into their credit card balance and try.

The district's hoteliers, with mark-ups of fifty per cent and often more, rubbed their hands and took the money. The customers, in general, were too intent on enjoying themselves and too keen on winning back some of their outlay at the races, to notice what they had spent. Everyone was happy. Everyone, it seems, gets something out of the week, right down to the enterprising residents near the course who have half-a-dozen cars parked in their back garden. They either have an awful lot of racegoing friends or a few pounds have been gratefully trousered in return for having to get the roller on the lawn next weekend.

Shops adorn their windows with suitable racing paraphernalia to attract the visitors, and the gift stores do particularly well at the end of the meeting. 'Conscience money, being spent on wives left at home,' one proprietor explained. But in the days prior to the invasion, the atmosphere slowly reaches its crescendo, until on Monday afternoon, come rain or shine, there is an unmistakeable tingle of excitement in the Cotswold air.

Mercy Rimell spent the week before Cheltenham trying to disguise the

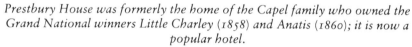

Prestbury House was formerly the home of the Capel family who owned the Grand National winners Little Charley (1858) and Anatis (1860); it is now a popular hotel.

fact that her world had temporarily been cut loose from its moorings.

The cause of her distress was the injury which had forced her to dramatically withdraw her champion hurdler Gaye Brief from his attempt to win the crown for the second successive year. Everyone in England, not least the bookmakers, had confidently expected Gaye Brief to win again. Everyone in Ireland believed Dawn Run could overturn the champion. Now, one of the most eagerly-awaited battles of the 1984 programme was pigeon-holed for at least a year, and Mercy – supposedly the iron lady of training – had, not for the first time, to hold her emotions in check.

It was far from being the first Cheltenham setback of her life. She had been too many times to the Festival to claim that, stretching way back to 1938 when she first accompanied husband Fred. He was a top jockey at the time, one of the very best and bravest in Britain indeed, and in 1945 he was to become one of only four men to ride four winners in a day at the course he had grown to love. By the following spring, when the National Hunt Festival came around again, he had an impressive total of forty-two winners at Cheltenham to his name. But he was to ride no more. In the Gold Cup that year he broke his neck for the second time, watched from the stands by Mercy.

'He had no option but to give up riding,' she recalls. 'He was in a plaster cast for six months, unable to do anything but sleep and eat. As he had been wasting to ride since the age of twelve, this part of the episode delighted him, and in those few months he began to put on a lot of weight. His natural weight had always been around 13 stone, yet I had known him ride at 10 stone 5 pounds.'

So T.F. Rimell disappeared forever from the jockeys' number-boards and began to appear, instead, among the trainers listed next to their runners in the morning papers. His enforced, premature diversion onto the other side of the racing road was to bring him more fame and success than even his riding had done. He had been champion jockey four times; now he was to become the first National Hunt trainer to win a million pounds in prize money for his owners. His big-race triumphs were regular – four Grand Nationals, two Gold Cups included – and, throughout it all, he retained a natural affection for the Cheltenham course, just a dozen or so miles away and across the M5 motorway from his stable-yard in the Worcestershire village of Kinnersley.

It was always said that Fred trained the horses so that they were ready to win, and Mercy found them the races to win. This was never a wife for decoration alone; Mrs Rimell played every bit as important a role in the success of the operation as her husband. A total of 158 winners trained at Cheltenham (second only to Fulke Walwyn, for whom he once rode), is testimony enough to the effectiveness of the team.

Fred Rimell - one of the great National Hunt trainers.

Mercy would ride out every morning on her wonderful hack Comedy of Errors, himself a Champion Hurdler, and then settle down to study the racing calendars, the form books and the entry lists. Her memory was, and still is, extraordinarily sharp, her habit of correcting those not as accurate as herself, quite unforgiving. But she was seldom wrong about a horse or the race in which it ought to run.

Suddenly, in the summer of 1981, Fred died. He left behind a string of talented horses and a widow who had either to take on the full responsibility for training them or get out of racing. She never even considered

Champion hurdlers after exercise at Kinnersley – Comedy of Errors and Gaye Brief. Comedy of Errors is now Mercy Rimell's hack and both horse and rider enjoy a gallop up the all-weather track after the string has finished work. Gaye Brief is being ridden by Cynthia Corbett who looks after him.

the second option. 'I suppose I thought I couldn't just sit around and vegetate,' she explains with typical practicality. 'So I gave it a try and, fortunately, the owners stood by me.'

She became the first lady of training and if, almost three years on, her position was under threat from the equally uncompromising, totally ambitious Jenny Pitman, there were no signs of any breakdown in the Rimell operation, nor of any decrease in Mercy's enthusiasm.

Her memory, certainly, was as good as ever. She was still putting me right every few minutes when I visited her rural mansion home on the hill above Upton-on-Severn, just before the Festival, and she still delighted in recounting famous Cheltenham victories from days gone by. None more so than the Gold Cup win of Royal Frolic in 1976.

'The horse belonged to Sir Edward Hanmer, who was really one of the old school, and could be fierce, even frightening at times. But he was getting to be a very old man – I think he was eighty-four that year – and it was partly that which persuaded me we should let his horse take his chance in the Gold Cup, even though he was inexperienced and only seven years old. Fred agreed and telephoned Sir Edward, who predictably said he thought it was a year too soon. Fred, trying to be tactful, said: "Aren't we running out of time?" I feared the worst, and apparently there was a long silence, but Sir Edward then gave a lovely chuckle, said "I suppose you're right" and agreed to let the horse run. It was as well that he did, because he died only a few months after seeing Royal Frolic win.'

That, however, was not the whole story. Mercy also remembered with total clarity the morning, weeks before the race, when she opened the *Sporting Life* in the stable office and cursed loudly at the odds quoted by a certain leading bookmaker on the Gold Cup. 'I couldn't believe it. Royal Frolic was 500-1 and a horse called Otter Way, a hunter-chaser if you please, was quoted at 100s. I turned to Kim Bailey, who was our assistant trainer at the time, and said: "How dare they quote a hunter-chaser shorter than us?" I hardly ever bet but Kim, myself and another lad were so incensed that we put £15 on between us. It turned out to be worth quite a lot of money!

'I think Royal Frolic's Gold Cup gave Fred more pleasure than any other race he ever won. He had bought the horse as an unbroken three-year-old, given him one run at four and then a year off. The Gold Cup was only the twelfth race of his career. Sir Edward's involvement made it all the better, because Fred had ridden for the Hanmer family for years.'

Mercy dresses as if for the cover of *Country Life* and contrives to look immaculate even on a rainswept day at Bangor-on-Dee. Yet in the eyes of many in the racing game, she remains stern and formidable, words she claims to detest and most definitely disown. She says she is essentially emotional, superstitious and sensitive, qualities that her detractors would not give her credit for. Her temperament can be thorny, I am sure she would concede that, but the fact remains that she is a different person away from the enforced rituals and postures of the racing day. At home, relaxed in a sweater and cords with one of her four dogs curled on her lap, another side of Mrs Rimell transpires.

'The press have always built me up as being tough and formidable,' she complains. 'They are saying similar nasty things now about Jenny Pitman, yet one never hears them said about Michael Dickinson, or Fred Winter. I don't like to say so, but I think it is a chauvinistic attitude which inspires these statements.

'In fact I am more sensitive than is good for me. I do get very upset about things sometimes, and people don't realise how hard it can be in this world for a woman left by herself. I found it horrifying to come to terms with that. I am not a social person, I've never played golf or bridge and I don't go out very much. So I find it very hard to get away from the job. I also happen to think it is more difficult for a woman to gain acceptance as a trainer than it is for a man. There are very good reasons for this – most owners are men, and many of them like to deal with other men. They like to go and have a chat, a drink and a joke with their trainer in the bar after a race. A woman seems a pretty poor substitute to some of them. So, while my owners have been marvellous and my staff have supported me wonderfully, it has been a taxing time since Fred died.'

Now, Gaye Brief or no Gaye Brief, Mercy was preparing for another crack at the meeting the Rimells always like to think of as their own. 'I look forward to the Festival very much. It is our local meeting, and the biggest of the year. To win a race there means more than anywhere else, with the exception of the National. But Cheltenham is a very tiring week too, especially for local trainers like myself. We are starting each day at home, as normal, and completing the regular routines before going to the course and doing battle with the crowds. It is hard getting around and I always see so many friends that I don't come across from one year to the next. People are always staying with me at the house. Dinner parties nearly every night. And still work to be done. It's very hectic.'

But Mercy relishes a battle and the Irish provide it every year at Cheltenham. 'It is a unique contest, not just horse against horse and trainer against trainer but also country against country. The Irish probably set themselves up for it even more than we do, because the prize money is exceptional by their standards, and frankly, I think they make the meeting what it is, with their enthusiasm and great competitive spirit. But that doesn't mean we are not trying very hard to beat them.'

A mere ten days before the Festival, Mercy was still confident of beating the Irish in at least one of the major events, as Gaye Brief's preparation went splendidly to plan. He had overcome his early-season hairline fracture of the near fore, emerged from the cloud which covered him after a controversial Christmas defeat at the hands of Dawn Run and suggested he was back at his best with a facile win in the Hereford hurdle race named, fittingly, after the man who bought him just before he died, Fred Rimell. Mercy herself ignored a bout of bronchitis to attend the early-morning gallops as usual and supervise the exercising of her champion. 'I am every bit as hopeful as I was last year,' she announced, having already stated publicly, 'Dawn Run will never beat us again.'

But on Sunday 4 March, Mercy had to tell the world that her horse had torn ligaments in his back and was out for the season. If it was not quite the end of the world it must fleetingly have seemed that way, as months of careful preparation, heartaches and hope, were all rendered useless. Dawn Run immediately went to odds-on in the betting and Mercy had to look forward to her favourite meeting without her favourite horse.

She had other runners, of course. And there were still people to see, jobs to be done, maybe even complaints to be made. Because Mercy, for one, did not much care for the new developments at Cheltenham, and she did not mind who knew. 'I have seen a great deal of changes there over the years,' she explained, 'and the course itself has undoubtedly changed for the better. But the stands, and general facilities for members, have not improved to keep in line with modern racing. The whole development has been done in a piecemeal fashion, and apparently without much logic. There are not enough places to sit down upstairs and I feel the whole thing leaves a good deal to be desired in terms of comfort. In fact, it's jolly uncomfortable. I also think some of the atmosphere has been lost around the unsaddling enclosure. Some may think it's all for the good, but I know plenty of old members who complain like mad and hate the changes.

'And as for the parade ring and the winners' enclosure overlapping, so that the runners for the next race have to walk round a white line like athletes, right behind the unsaddling ... well, it might be all right for Sedgefield or Fakenham, but not Cheltenham, surely.' Mercy gave a sharp shake of her impeccably coiffured head, drew haughtily on her French cigarette and then, quite unexpectedly, giggled. 'They won't like me saying that, will they?' 'They' probably would not, but then neither would they be entirely surprised. Mrs Mercy Rimell of Kinnersley has never, after all, been the retiring type of female keen to shelter behind someone else's skirts and speak only when spoken to. If she has strong views, others will hear them. It has sometimes made her unpopular, created dragonesque impressions in suspicious minds and led many to file her under the category 'dangerous – do not approach', which is a pity. Prickly and intolerant though she can be, there really is another side to Mercy, a side she seldom shows on the racecourse, where her defences are raised automatically. It manifests itself when she talks of her first equine loves, the gymkhana and showing worlds, a world which still enthrals and entices her now. She judges at horse shows, and is proud of the fact that her twelve-year-old grandson has already won events. They rate a long way from Cheltenham in sporting importance but then, to Mercy, racing is the business end of her life with horses, and the two must never be confused.

Kinnersley is a mere hamlet and Upton-on-Severn is hardly the hub of the industrial nation, but Mercy Rimell almost lives in the big city compared to the base of her fellow trainer, Michael Scudamore. He actually lives in the neighbouring county of Herefordshire and is only a forty-minute motorway dash from the Cheltenham course, but you would never know it by the utter solitude of his home and yard atop a hill outside the village of Hoarwithy.

Mike and his wife Mary live in a three hundred-year-old beamed farmhouse. Some of the stables in which he runs his ambitious but still small-time business were converted from ancient stone barns. The green and pleasant fields of the Welsh border country run away from the property and it is the type of place where one could spend all day sitting at the lounge window gazing at the scenery. The Scudamores are content and Mike, though still occasionally regretful over the fall which forced him into premature retirement from the saddle, has his memories as well as his hopes. He rode the Gold Cup winner in 1957, the same year he married Mary and moved to Hoarwithy. He has also trained a winner at the Cheltenham Festival – the wonderfully consistent Fortina's Palace. His Cheltenham record, in short, is impressive and he, quite naturally, loves the place like a second home.

Peter Scudamore would dearly love to have a similar affection for what is very much his local course. But Michael's son, number one jockey to the David Nicholson yard at Condicote, had still never ridden a Festival winner, despite winning the jockeys' championship at a precocious twenty-three and finishing second on three further occasions. It was an omission which nagged at his active, intelligent mind and, up till then, had not permitted him to enjoy the Festival in quite the way that his father had done as a rider and still managed to do as a trainer.

Father and son approached the '84 meeting in their very different ways. Mike was planning to run Fred Pilliner, a horse named after a loyal but tragic stud groom who died of cancer without ever seeing his namesake run. 'Fred', bred on the premises by the Scudamores and very much a family favourite, had already won six chases during the season and was now aimed at the Ritz Club Chase on the final day of the programme. Peter was booked to ride the horse, and what a way to end the jinx it would be if he was to win on his father's one Festival runner. Michael daydreamed of it happening that way. Peter hardly dared think about it. But, now twenty-five and established among the country's top three riders, he had a diary bursting with promising rides for the Festival and anyone making a book on him breaking his duck would surely have made it an odds-on chance.

Still, he fretted about it. Intense, sometimes sensitive, always progressive in his thinking, he was – in the words of his father – 'far more professional in his attitude than most of the jockeys of my day, myself included'. Peter saw it like this: 'Maybe I put pressure on myself, but if you go several years without riding a winner at a meeting as big as this, people begin to talk about it and that just adds to the problem. For the past three years I have been involved with Broadsword, who was a

Peter Scudamore, number one jockey to David Nicholson and still waiting for his first win at a Festival meeting.

brilliant hurdler but just got beaten in both the Triumph Hurdle and the Champion Hurdle. When he was second in the Champion in 1982 I sulked. I went home and watched the video time after time, not wanting to eat or talk. I was bad company – a bad loser in some ways. I blamed myself, you see. Now that Broadsword has retired I feel a weight lifted from me, because he was always expected to win. If I can win on anything over the three days now, though, it will be an even bigger relief.'

Michael said he was 'pleased and proud' about Peter. He was too sensible a father to gush any more. Instead, with that craggy face set into the half-smile of nostalgia, he recounted how Fortina's Palace had come along to virtually save him from an early grave as a trainer. 'A fellow called Jack Davis often used to come here fishing. He stayed in the village and came up here to look at the horses, but times were tough and I really didn't have much worth looking at. One day he said to me: "You can't win races with that lot. Come on, we'll go to Ireland and buy something decent." So we bought Fortina's Palace, who won thirteen times, including the Grand Annual at the Festival. It got me off the ground as a trainer. I've a lot to thank Jack for.'

Without much hesitation, Michael names that Grand Annual win as the biggest thrill of his training career. He explains it in a way which paraphrases the entire concept of the Festival: 'It's our cup final, isn't it? It's the Wembley of our world, where all the work and the slog of the season, through good weather and bad, finally reaches its climax. And with the Irish there, friendly in rivalry but absolutely determined to take home all the pots, there somehow seems more point to it all than there is at a normal meeting.

'When I had to give up riding, I missed the atmosphere of Cheltenham as much as anything. Liverpool might have affected me more – I was like a little boy at Christmas every year for the National – but Cheltenham still had that excitement stretching right through the week, like no other meeting in the country. Every race was a big one, and at the end of each day we jockeys used to congregate in the cellar bar, sit on champagne cases and talk our way through the day, race by race, while we downed a few bottles. It was a magical week. It still is, of course, but as a trainer, it isn't quite the same. I envy Peter for what he's got in store next week, I really do. Whether he wins or not, I hope he enjoys it.'

If Scudamore junior was wondering where his first Festival winner would come from, imagine the feelings of his guv'nor, David Nicholson. He had held a trainer's licence since 1968 and had turned out more placed horses at Cheltenham than he cared to relate. But not one Festival winner.

Like Scudamore, Nicholson had a famous father to follow, in his case a man for whom hardly any glory at Cheltenham had been barred. 'Frenchie' won every race open to him on the Festival card during his riding career, then won a few more as a trainer. With the racecourse virtually an extension of his back garden, he was the local squire, and as his son fondly recalls: 'Father was a very popular character around Prestbury and I'm told that in 1942 – when I was only three – he told just about everyone in the village that he would win the Gold Cup on Médoc. There was something close to hysteria when he did it, just as he said he would, and I can only imagine the goings-on in the local pubs that night.'

David – 'the Duke' to all in racing for his sometimes lordly manner – moved with the family to Cheltenham when he was six months old, lived there for twenty-two years and still considers it very much his home town. He first went to the Festival in 1946 and recalls that a much greater percentage of the crowd tended to watch racing from the middle of the course in those far-off, pound-stretching days. 'The town was alive with racing then, much more so than it is now, but then I guess people just didn't have so much to do with their leisure time soon after the war and the entertainments which were available naturally became more important and more talked-about.'

One of David's less-known landmarks was riding Dorothy Paget her last winner before she died, when the great lady's horses were almost all stabled with Frenchie. But, as he says: 'I always had training in mind – but I imagined I would have ten or a dozen horses, not upwards of sixty as I've got now.'

The label of gallant bridesmaid which has been attached to Broadsword, the best horse he has trained, still plainly affronts Nicholson. Defeat hurt him as much, if not more than it hurt his jockey Scudamore, but his outlook as he approached yet another Festival with yet another clutch of runners was nothing if not phlegmatic. 'Yes, it's frustrating not to have had a winner at Cheltenham but really I'm happy to get my horses there after such a long season. Broadsword went there three years in succession and was always in the frame. Goldspun has been twice and now he's going back a third time. We've planned his entire season around the Festival and he is perhaps my number one hope.'

Such optimism would have brought comfort to Goldspun's owner, who happened to be yet another of the unlucky men still without a March meeting winner despite many valiant attempts. He also happened to be a director of the Cheltenham course, which only made his frustration more acute, and one of the richest and most influential of National Hunt racing's patrons.

Lord (Sam) Vestey has owned horses since the age of twenty-one, and Frenchie Nicholson trained him his first winner at Cheltenham's April meeting of 1964. But in the twenty years which followed he had failed to strike at the Festival.

There was not much likelihood of him falling out with his trainer over the issue, having been a close friend of David Nicholson since their pony club days. They even share a March birthday. A combined first Festival winner for them would be every bit as fitting as the Scudamores linking up in victory and to the sporting peer – a Cheltenham steward since 1971 and a director since 1976 – the meaning of it was quite plain. 'It is quite simply that National Hunt racing is one of my favourite hobbies and its mecca is the National Hunt meeting,' he explained. 'To win any race at the Festival, where you are competing against the very cream of the world's hurdlers and chasers, must be a wonderful experience.'

It was Lord Vestey's greatest wish to win the Gold Cup, the race which, he says, 'brings a lump to your throat just watching them going down at the start', but he would settle for very much less exalted victories and The Duke hoped to provide them. All parties admitted, however, that it seemed more likely this year that a Festival win would go to brother Mark Vestey. He had only ever owned two horses, as opposed to the scores owned by his brother, but the second of them, Voice of Progress, was a major Nicholson hope in the Arkle Chase on day one. This, too, would be a win tinged with sadness, because a riding accident had confined Mark Vestey to a wheelchair only months previously, and he would not be present at headquarters to see his young 'chaser tackle his biggest test. But Lord Vestey would be there and you could be sure he would break off from the multitude of duties incumbent on a Board member at the Festival to watch his brother's horse run with at least as much enthusiasm and hope as he watched his own. It would not just be for family sympathy, either. It simply characterises the Vestey spirit, the National Hunt spirit. Few do it better.

Lord Vestey's direct responsibility as a director is for the upkeep of the buildings and not least for the provision of lavatories at the race-course. He spends time each year inspecting every male and female lavatory, checking that the chains pull and seeing whether the pans need renewing!

Edward Gillespie, the racecourse manager, was approaching his fourth Festival meeting as one who believes he knows what to expect, thinks he can handle it but fears constantly that the totally unexpected might happen. 'There is only so much you can do, so many contingencies you can plan for. Once you think you have all your options covered, you just have to hope for the best.'

For an unusually young man at the helm of a traditionally middle-aged and older ship, Gillespie had achieved wonders in gaining the complete confidence of his Board. He confirmed: 'It would be very frustrating to have directors who were constantly vetoing all my proposals. But they are very progressive in their views – trying to take the entertainment to the public rather than sitting back and taking no part in the process.' As he spoke, he was surrounded by evidence of his testimony, boxes full of the latest lines in Cheltenham merchandise. Ash trays, beer mugs, champagne flutes, drinks mats, postcards and port decanters, all adorned with the crest of the Steeplechase Company, were ready for distribution to various selling-points around the course. Some might think that it was asking a little too much to expect the average punter, having forked out £20 for his club badge, possibly the same again on food and drink and heaven knows how much on betting, to then dig even deeper in his ever-lightening wallet and hand over £20 for a pack of six drinks mats, no matter how attractive the pictures of the racecourse on them might be. But the merchandise market had proved strong in other sports, notably golf, tennis and cricket, and it was typical of Gillespie's enterprise that he should wish to introduce it at Cheltenham, typical of his Board that they had rubber-stamped the proposal rather than talked all round it, deferred a decision for twelve months and passed round their own port decanter instead.

Gillespie and his team had already been spectacularly successful as salesmen. The ninety-five boxes and luncheon rooms in the grandstand and eighty-nine chalets in the tented village (sixteen extra had been fitted in when it was clear the original number was wholly inadequate) had all been booked months before and the waiting list of companies eager to entertain on the course and willing to pay £5,000 for the privilege had now stretched to seventy names. Now, in the few days left before the event began, Gillespie and his staff would have to cope with dozens of phone calls from harassed secretaries and confused executives wishing to check arrangements for their prize clients.

It would not only be the business customers who took up the time of the Cheltenham office staff, however. Secretary Rosemary Hammond would testify to the fact that individuals can be just as problematical. It is Mrs Hammond who is responsible for handling every one of the application forms for badges that flop onto the doormat of the Prestbury Park offices, and if that does not sound too arduous a task it immediately becomes clear just how hard it is to satisfy the requirements of every member when one reads a small selection of the letters, or hangs around the office long enough – normally no more than five minutes at this time of year – to catch one of the phone calls of complaint or confused enquiry. Frankly, Mrs Hammond's job requires the patience of an extremely tolerant saint.

'People think we have a vast team of people armed with computers, ready to deal with their enquiries. But this is all there is,' explained Rosemary with a telling glance round the tiny club office. Her end of the room, partitioned off by a row of filing cabinets, contained a desk, currently covered with application forms, and some shelves. Beyond the cabinets, genial Betty Hale operated the switchboard: 'We have five lines and they ring non-stop this week. We did have an extra line put on, but we eventually found it was ringing out in the luncheon room on the new stand, so I don't know how many callers thought we were all having a day off!'

Rosemary freely admits that all she knows about horses could be written on the back of a postage stamp. The racing is not her job. 'We do anything and everything else, though, from sorting out the VIPs with the best treatment to rushing about getting toilet rolls.'

Cheltenham Racecourse directors and staff, September 1984.

Seated left to right: *Richard Wasley (Company Secretary), Kathie Pope (Accounts), Edward Gillespie (General Manager), Bryan Robinson (Director), Miles Gosling (Chairman), Piers Bengough (Director), Tommy Wallis (Managing Director RHT), Philip Arkwright (Clerk of the Course), Betty Hale (Secretary), Rosemary Hammond (Club Secretary), David Ayres (Accounts Clerk).*
Standing left to right: *Margaret Rabjohns, Elsie O'Dea, Joyce Sexton, Olive Fitzharris, Joan Murphy, Janet Farley, Frank Jones, Bill Wilson, Ned Nugent, Phil Hatcher, John Newth, Keith Jones, Phil Holland, Paul Townley, Bob Galpin, Scat Williams, Martin Nugent, Mick Williams.*
Missing from this picture are: *Lord Vestey (Director), Charles Hambro (Director), George Excell, Dave Pockett.*

It was to be her third Festival and, when the first day arrived, she would pick up her books and bags and move camp, restationing herself behind a counter at the main members' entrance. There, apart from dealing with general enquiries and helping to distribute ordered but uncollected badges, she would assist in the supervision of the anti-gatecrasher operation. 'Some people will try anything to get in without paying,' she explains. 'Those who are experts will choose a moment when the gateman at his entrance is arguing with somebody else and then slip behind him. That sort are difficult to catch if they time it right, and I have no doubt some are successful. But others try all kinds of outrageous things. A favourite is to turn up at the stables gate with a bucket and sponge, trying to pass off as a stable-lad. Last year there was even one little man who presented himself there in jockeys' silks and claimed he was riding in the next race and had just slipped out to his car to collect his horse's passport. The gatemen understandably didn't believe him and he was kept there for a long while, getting steadily more harassed. It turned out he was telling the truth!'

Rosemary's problems, she pointed out with some foreboding, had hardly begun. Philip Arkwright's greatest worry looked like being lifted as Friday dawned bright and sunny and each succeeding call he put in to the local weather centre offered nothing more threatening than the occasional isolated wintry shower over the coming three days. 'We've got good ground at the moment,' he reported, 'and I wouldn't at all mind starting the meeting today. Everything essential has been done out on the course and Phil Hatcher's men are now onto the "could be dones". By Monday they will be coping only with anything that goes wrong – and something, right up to the last minute, always does.'

Chapter 8

IT RAINED HEAVILY IN Cheltenham on Sunday night. Coming a bare thirty-six hours before the Festival, that would normally be enough to send the entire racecourse staff into a communal gloom and hurry those with weak constitutions in the direction of the tranquillisers. But not this year. When Monday dawned, dull but dry, it found Philip Arkwright doing his rounds of the course complete with stick, cap, tweeds and the jaunty expression of one who had no cares in the world. Which was not, of course, strictly true. The Major, however, was contentedly unconcerned about the weather.

'We had a quarter-of-an-inch last night,' he beamed, 'which was just right. I know it's not often I would say that the day before the Festival, but for a change we needed a little rain. If we have no more the ground will be perfect and I defy any trainer to find an excuse for their horse.'

At lunchtime it started to snow, but even that failed to dispirit the management team. This time it was Edward Gillespie who glanced out of the office window at the gently falling flakes and muttered: 'Good. Everyone will know the Festival is about to start now.' Not that it seemed many were in doubt, judging by the manager's fruitless attempts to escape from the telephone switchboard in the short while it took Betty to collect her snack lunch. At least two lines were constantly ringing and Edward, clipped, precise but never impolite, managed to answer no less than fifteen enquiries in the space of five and a half minutes. Most people wanted to know how much they would have to pay for a ticket, some were unsure whether there would be any left and a few called with more outlandish questions, such as whether they could bring their dog along. Edward's eyebrows shot upwards at each odd variation on a familiar theme, but treated them all with the deference of a diplomat.

He was well used to the novice racegoer and his whims. Indeed, he appeared to have made something of a study of the species. 'You can always tell the people who only come racing once a year,' he explained. 'Watch them arrive in the car park. They will get out of their cars wearing totally unsuitable clothing. The chap who knows Cheltenham of old will wear mackintosh, trousers and flat hat, whatever the weather – and much the same clothing applies to the ladies. But those who have not been before arrive in stiletto heels and glamorous hats and are next seen creeping back to their car after the second race to put on wellingtons.

'But the beauty of it is,' he went on with the sudden air of a salesman, 'we have no area restricted to people who are knighted, or even to those who have lots of money. It's a total mix. At Royal Ascot, some people go just because they want to dress up; others go because they want to watch them dress up and the rest go for the racing. I think you can be sure that the vast majority of the crowds at Cheltenham come to watch the racing.'

There were, as usual, no worries about the quality in that regard. The fields had by now been declared for the opening day of the programme and, if the Waterford Crystal Champion Hurdle undoubtedly suffered from the absence of the Champion, there were several cracking contests to whet the appetite, notably an Anglo-Irish duel of potentially epic proportions in the Arkle Chase between Noddy's Ryde (for England) and Bobsline (for Ireland). The first batch of Irish horses and their handlers had been due to arrive late on Friday night but, owing to transportation difficulties, it was past midnight on Sunday before the stable-staff were occupied with inmates. Now, however, the boxes were beginning to fill quite

An important part of any weighing room is the tea bar!

rapidly, and already a short, orderly line of horseboxes from farflung parts like Dumfries and Dundalk were assembled on the gravel car park outside the fence guarding the security-conscious stable area.

But it was not so much the course, the runners or the stables which concerned Cheltenham's manager on this eve-of-meeting, but such widely unconsidered matters as toilet facilities for the tented village, the working of the lifts in the new stand and the car parking provision for expected VIPs. These, plus a few dozen other minor essentials, made up his cluttered programme until the crowds began to invade before midday on Tuesday, but he still found time to laugh at himself over a hastily-swallowed plate of roast beef at the traditional pre-Festival lunch for staff. 'In the week before the March meeting, I have to make so many little trips around the course, normally to the tented village but sometimes to the boxes in the stand or to the banqueting rooms, that I usually drive the car. More than once, I have found myself sidetracked, gone on somewhere else by foot and then totally forgotten where I'd left the car and had to waste several minutes searching for it.'

The tented village was his pride and joy, and it looked a picture. Neat name boards outside each chalet announced the identity of those who would soon be wining and dining on carpeted, raised floorboards in surroundings hardly in keeping with the time-honoured conception of tents. There were marketing companies, builders, television companies, the odd private club and a few individual trainers – messrs Walwyn and Nicholson plus Mrs Rimell – taking advantage of the chance to entertain their owners and maybe woo a potential new one or two.

Chris Coley, a Cheltenham businessman, is one of those responsible for selling the space to companies and as he busied himself around the site, checking for the umpteenth time that his clients would find TV sets, bar space and dining tables all in pristine shape, he remarked: 'This event has taken off in the past few years. I am bringing twelve hundred businessmen this year, over the course of the three days – and that makes it a very big event for business entertainment.'

Manager Gillespie came up with the statistic that, if the tube frames of the tented village were laid end to end, they would measure eleven miles. The way things are progressing, they might stretch from Cheltenham to London in a few years' time.

The first panic of Festival week had already been faced and overcome by the time the staff sat down to their informal Monday lunch. It had been nothing trivial. The Prestbury Suite, banqueting centre for the course, might just have burned to the ground at breakfast time.

At 8.30am, one of the catering staff on early duty detected a strange smell in the suite's dining room. He went to investigate and found the

The 'doughnut man' at work.

room full of smoke. Summoning help, which arrived in the shape of more staff bearing fire extinguishers, he finally discovered that the cause of the potential inferno had been a spotlight facing inwards onto a plastic coated wooden screen. The screen burned darkly and then caught light. Given a few minutes more, the whole room could have been blazing merrily and someone would have had to paint an apologetic sign telling the members they could not sit down to lunch on Champion Hurdle day. They would not have been amused.

By lunchtime the drama was a laughing matter, even if the humour was tinged with the uncomfortable knowledge of what might have been. One crisis was passed. Perhaps things could only get better. That, in any case, was the attitude of John Urquhart and Bob Dalgetty, travelling troubleshooters for Letherby & Christopher, caterers to Cheltenham racecourse since the initial Gold Cup in 1924. 'This meeting is never dull,' explained Mr Urquhart, the director of customer relations. 'Now and again it can be amusing – although the things which happen to us are normally funnier to look back on than they are at the time!'

It was the Scottish-born Dalgetty who painted the most vivid picture of the catering operation at the Festival. 'It is like fighting a war knowing only you can win,' he said. 'We approach it with determination and it is bloody hard work. Afterwards, there is a type of jetlag to be suffered. We all feel drained and empty.'

Catering is probably the most surprising area of the entire Festival mechanism. The scale of it is quite staggering, certainly beyond the imagination of the haggard, beaten punter chewing on his burger in the silver ring, or the mink-and-diamond-bedecked female delicately nibbling lobster in a private box in the new stand.

Figures do not tell the entire story but some are worth relating. Like the fact that five thousand lunches will be served on each day of the meeting, that the solid intake will include around twelve thousand hamburgers and the liquid intake a small matter of six thousand bottles of champagne and seventy thousand bottles of beer. But it is no use having the edibles without the staff to serve them, and in addition to eighty of their permanent staff of one hundred and twenty turning up for the frenzied Cheltenham week, L&C hire no fewer than eleven hundred casual staff to man their sixty-five public selling points around the course. They do not escape with simply paying them a fee for the week, either. Beds in the Cheltenham area have to be found for all the casual staff, who travel up from the company's Ascot base, and for around three hundred of the casuals. As anyone who has tried to book a hotel room for himself and his wife during Festival week will appreciate, this in itself is an awesome task. Many of the barmaids, indeed, are found lodgings in private houses for the duration, but John Urquhart reports that even this can cost the company more than £20 per person per night. Not even the private landlord wants to miss out on the annual goldrush. Staff also stay in local village halls and skittle alleys, in both of which a surprising number of camp beds are erected.

The planning, clearly, is not done in a week. Bob Dalgetty explains: 'We start our work on the next Festival two weeks after the previous one – and it would be sooner but we all need that two week break to get over it. Our first job is to book hotel accommodation for the managers and senior staff so that they won't be left on the streets. By October each year, six months before the event, we have started to get our menus costed and planned, after which we order the food and equipment necessary to provide them. At the end of February, with a fortnight to go, we feel we are in trouble if all the administration is not complete.

'There are almost as many jokes about racecourse catering as there are about mothers-in-law,' added Urquhart. 'Sometimes I feel like rising to the bait when I hear them because I know they give a false impression. But it really isn't worth it. The standard of the food now is unrecognisable from years gone by, and another thing worth saying – which will surprise many people – is that we do not slip a few pence, or even pounds on the cost of everything for an event like Cheltenham. Our prices are standard for a year at a time, which probably makes us the only business in the town not to increase them this week!'

Both Bob Dalgetty and John Urquhart have racing in their blood, which is valuable to their employers even if it leaves them both frustrated that they are unable to join the crowds watching the racing. Dalgetty's father is a permit-holding trainer and Urquhart, whose family used to farm in the Cheltenham area, owns racehorses himself, including the useful Dargai, who had won three times in the season when we talked. He stays with his mother for the Festival, and has been coming to the meeting since 1953.

'Our company's attitude is that we are part of racing,' says Urquhart. 'We do the catering at twelve courses now.' Dalgetty interjects: 'Small enough to care and big enough to cope. That could be our motto. We understand what racing people want, and how quickly they want it. Owners and trainers, the press and the punters all have different demands for us to cope with – and then there are the company executives here to entertain. Racing is a tremendously important business selling medium these days, and we have a part to play in that.'

Their part was to supervise the smooth running of the tented village. 'It makes it our most difficult operation – not as big as Royal Ascot, perhaps, but then they don't have a tented village. The people in there have paid a lot of money and don't want camp-fire food. They expect high standards and they must get it, no matter how difficult it may be.'

The camp-fire analogy was surprisingly accurate. Those of the fifty duty chefs at Cheltenham who found themselves attached to the chalet area were not quite provided with the most modern of equipment. Stationed at the back of the compound, out of sight of the well-dressed diners and looking almost bizarre in their chef's hats, they did their cooking on army-style calor-gas stoves. They were not expected to moan, even if the weather turned nasty, as it has a habit of doing during the second week of March.

Just as the elements present a perennial nightmare to Philip Arkwright, so they take Letherby and Christopher into the worrying unknown. The uncertainty can turn out to be extremely expensive – the food has to be ordered and on site whatever the weather forecast. If a day's racing is lost, so is a great deal of grub. Bob Dalgetty clearly remembers 1978, when the Gold Cup programme was abandoned due to heavy overnight falls of snow. But then he would – it was the day he joined the company. At least no such traumas were on the immediate horizon this year.

It is the resident manager of the catering outfit at Cheltenham, who holds the entire operation together in Festival week, while Dalgetty and

Urquhart, armed with one each of the forty walkie-talkie radio sets used by the company, prowl potential trouble areas. Inside the Prestbury Suite itself, a computer registers all the credit bookings. It has been brought up for the week from the Ascot base and no-one dares to imagine the chaos if it malfunctioned. Half of the company's accounts staff are on hand, however, to cope with the mounds of paperwork which accumulate by the hour.

On Monday morning of Festival week, John Urquhart calls all the staff together for a briefing on customer relations. This, he says, is one of the most important hours of the week because it can remind everyone of their responsibilities. Many is the time I have been discouraged from returning to one racecourse bar or another by the surly or downright rude attitude of the staff. I must say it has never happened at Cheltenham, and Urquhart says: 'We largely employ people who have worked here before, which is a help, but everyone is told that the customer is here to enjoy himself and they should do everything possible to make sure he does. They must be cheerful, quick and slick. The barmaids, at least, are more like hostesses.'

The turnover is vast, from the popular and mass-produced hot roast beef sandwiches at £2 a time up to the costliest bottle of vintage brandy, on sale at £380. As ever at such an event, there is temptation in the way of staff, but light-fingered types are summarily dealt with. 'We have sacked people during this meeting before,' warned Urquhart, 'from the lowest of menial staff to one in a very senior position indeed. It doesn't matter who you are – dishonesty cannot be tolerated.'

Security is just one of the problems for the catering chiefs. Over the week to come, they knew their wit, patience, stamina and ingenuity would be tested to the full, and that it would leave them exhausted when it was all over. As John Urquhart said, picking up his radio, donning his overcoat and preparing for the fray: 'You go home after this meeting and it is like coming back from the war. For a few days, you just can't talk about sensible, reasonable things.'

Major Arkwright set out on his second course inspection of the day at 3pm. It was dry now, but grey and bleak, with a wind that might have come straight from the arctic whipping down off Cleeve Hill. Much more like proper Cheltenham weather than all that fancy sunshine of the previous few days.

The traditional excitement of the day had not passed by the clerk of the course, despite his experience. Although everyone employed on the course was working at full stretch on final preparations, they almost all without exception wore the bright smiles usually adopted by children on Christmas Eve. It might be the busiest week of the year but it was plainly also the most enjoyable, and a twinkle of anticipated pleasure was plainly detectable in Philip Arkwright's eyes as we walked briskly away from the stands, pausing by each obstacle so that he could inspect the construction for any improbable defects, lingering longest over the one fence newly-built for this year's Festival. 'They have a three-year life and are replaced on a rota system. Our fence-maker is a deceptively young looking character named George Excell. He's a master craftsman at this business but well past retirement age. On 1 January each year I say, "Well, George, what are we going to do this time?" and he always gives the same reply. "I might give it one more go, sir," he will say, and you know he can't bear to give it up.'

Cheltenham demands more maintenance work than other jumping courses because it has twenty-four fences instead of the customary ten and seventeen hurdles rather than the regular six or seven. There are two separate courses, the new and the old, a system created because one could not be guaranteed capable of taking three days' racing in March if the weather was bad.

Philip clicked his tongue over the new housing development on the town centre side of the course and wondered idly if it was really an eyesore from the stand or if no-one ever noticed things like that. He pointed out the brook which runs down the centre of the course, out of sight from the main viewing areas, and the helicopter pad which would be heavily engaged in twenty-four hours time. Colt Aviation run a shuttle service by helicopter to the nearby Staverton Airport and the system is increasingly popular with the sort of racegoer who likes to do things in comfort and does not have to check his bank balance before setting out.

We arrived back to the lights and comforting warmth of the office block and Philip gave me a viewing of his living quarters for the next four days. They did not amount to much – a narrow, hospital-style bed in the ambulance room, covered by rubber, waterproof sheets ('very sweaty and uncomfortable'), with a single, upright wooden chair on which to stack his clothes. 'The bed is not up to Ritz standards,' Philip confessed, 'but in terms of a going report it is "firm but level", and there is a very good reason for me wishing to use it. I learned my lesson six years ago.'

The episode to which the Major referred was a classic clerk's dilemma, one which had left a lasting impression on him and instilled a sense of caution which explained his settling for the spartan conditions of the ambulance room each Festival time.

For the 1978 Festival, he had spent Monday and Tuesday nights at the course, on hand in case of emergencies through bad weather or other unforeseen elements. But on the Wednesday night he chose to go home. 'The decision may have been influenced by the fact that the first two days had gone well – perhaps too well,' he recalls. 'By 7pm preparations for the following day were complete. I had a last word with Phil Hatcher and then made a final call to the Met Office, who predicted a mild night, with a fine but cold Gold Cup day. There seemed no obvious reason why I should spend another night away, so around 8pm, I climbed into my car for the forty-mile drive home to Swalcliffe, near Banbury.'

He opted out of a dinner party which his wife was attending and went to bed early, leaving a note to the effect that he should be woken in the improbable event of some dramatic change in the weather. Otherwise, his alarm was scheduled to sound at 5.30am and he planned to be back on the course by 7. It was just before 2am when Mrs Arkwright arrived home and, as the weather was still perfectly fine, she did not disturb her slumbering husband. 'But an hour after that,' recalls Philip with the horror of a relived nightmare, 'and for what reason I shall never know, I woke up anyway. I could hear no rain beating against my bedroom window but I wasn't content. There was an eerie kind of stillness of a sort which, in my experience, only means one thing. I tottered to the window and had my worst fears realised – snow was falling in a solid blanket.'

The panic of the soldier who has left his post at just the moment when the invasion takes place must have overtaken Major Arkwright at that moment. He remembers it was only a matter of minutes before he was on the road, hastily dressed and washed, and that despite the ungodly hour and the unforgiving crisis, he was thinking clearly enough to take a route which avoided the Cotswold villages at high risk of being cut off by the blizzard's residue, and that by 4.30am he had slithered and crawled his way to Northleach. He thought his troubles were over – just a few minutes more and he would be on the outskirts of Cheltenham. 'It was then that I saw the lorry on the hill in front of me – jack-knifed right across the road.'

He managed to find a telephone and put in a call to the Chairman of the Steeplechase Company, who thought he was the victim of a practical joke. Colonel Piers Bengough, deputy Senior Steward for the day, was then woken and needed much persuasion from the harassed Major before accepting his story of events. Whether or not he looked out of his window to confirm the rumour, he agreed to leap in his Land Rover and head for the course, ready to take the necessary steps to abandon the card.

Philip then had his one piece of luck. Emerging from the phone box he saw the equivalent of an oasis to a man marooned in a desert. Except it was no mirage – the flashing orange light just down the road really was a gritting lorry. By dint of more persuasion, and the happy coincidence that the driver was Irish and had been shouting Monksfield to the Champion Hurdle only half-a-day earlier, he then had a trail of grit to follow

The Irish arriving at the racecourse stables on Sunday afternoon before the start of the Festival. The horses have been unloaded and now it is the turn of the tack, food, rugs etc.

all the way to Prestbury Park. As he got there he made a mental note. Three nights putting up with solitude and stiffness were very much preferable to what he had just been through.

'So I've stayed here every year since,' he concluded. 'But even here I have had one unforeseen panic. I woke at dead of night during the Festival one year and, through bleary eyes, peered through the curtain. My heart went into my mouth when I saw the windows were white with what could only be snow ... then I remembered. The ambulance room windows were painted white and the illusion of snow was caused by paint having chipped away.'

Hong Kong's two ultra-modern racetracks both boast huge electronic scoreboards which flash up the outrageously large number of dollars gambled on each race. Fantasy running amok, it occurred to me that it might be illuminating to erect a similar board in the middle of Cheltenham the day before the March meeting, giving a running total of how much money has been brought into the area for this one, crazy week. It would need to cope with a lot of digits.

Most of the cash which arrives is meant for betting. But not necessarily on the races. Plenty of the punters who pour into the town come intent on spending every waking hour gambling, and as the horses are disobliging enough to confine their activities to the afternoons, that leaves time for diversification. The gaming clubs of Bristol pick up extra business with an Irish accent. But still the appetite of the gambler is unsatisfied. So he plays cards, anywhere it is legal and – if local legend is to be believed – in plenty of illegal spots, too.

The police believe they have the problem under control. Their spokesman said: 'We enforce the law against gambling in public places. I'm not saying it doesn't go on, but if they play cards for money in their own hotel rooms, that is out of our jurisdiction.' But Edward Gillespie has heard different: 'There is apparently a travelling gambling school which moves around Cheltenham in race week, turning up in unlikely places such as Greek restaurants. They are always one step ahead of the police. Some people will gamble on anything, and this is just a natural progression from what goes on at racing.'

Despite the mysterious nocturnal activities around the area, the great majority of punting is still done on the racecourse – and here, Gillespie was able to speak from first-hand experience. 'We have seen people getting out of their Rolls-Royces in the car park, stripping off the inside of the door and taking out wads of notes. People like this bring a quite phenomenal amount of money to the races. Of course, there are others who come racing and spend no money at all.'

The latter category are thin on the ground in Festival week, and among the Irish invaders, the non-spender is non-existent. Provision is made for the excesses of the visitors: Irish banks open mobile offices on the course and great business is done, refilling the wallets of those whose luck was down the previous day. Some bookmakers treble their usual staff to cope with the rush and still find themselves overrun all afternoon and utterly exhausted by evening.

Bill Kendrick, whose bookmaking firm occupies the number one pitch in Tattersalls at Cheltenham, describes the Irish punters as 'absolutely fearless. If they fancy a horse, they back it. They treat it as a huge holiday. They come over to gamble and, so long as they have a good time they are happy – win, lose or draw.' Like most bookies at Cheltenham, Kendrick has a tale or two to tell about the droves of Irish priests who come over for the meeting, some of them behaving in a manner most of us would consider distinctly unholy. His favourite is of a day when he was surrounded by ten men of the cloth. He recalls: 'They couldn't decide which horse they liked. Finally, one of them took out a bible and said he was going to look upstairs for some inspiration.' Message received, the horse was chosen and duly backed. He fell at the second fence. I doubt if it weakened the priests' faith one bit – they would have been back in time for another tilt at the next event. I once saw a priest celebrating a win at the Festival with all the exaggerated passion of a footballer who had just scored at Wembley. Dressed in black robes and dog-collar, scorning the escape of a disguise, he leaped high in the air, slapped the hands of his companion in the manner made famous by Caribbean cricketers and then set off at a sprint towards the ring, yelping like an over-excited dog. I wondered briefly what advice he would give at confession the following week to those of his flock who came seeking forgiveness for blowing the housekeeping money at the races!

I noticed the difference as soon as I arrived at the swing doors. The Queens Hotel was not what it had been.

The paintings had disappeared from the walls. The restaurant had been gutted of its fine, period furniture and filled with iron-backed garden chairs. An extra bar had been built. And the foyer, customarily all plush and hush, was littered with men dressed in a way the Queens would frown on, fifty-one weeks of the year. There was a preponderance of braces, belts, open-necked shirts and thick walking sticks on show. The buzz around the room was of a distinct tone. Virtually every accent was Irish. The invasion had begun in earnest.

It was tea-time Monday and the hotel's newly-registered residents were killing time before the first of the night's glasses of stout slipped down. The chat was inevitably racing and gambling, the tone coarse but the excitement unmistakeable. While they waited like greyhounds in the traps, the staff hustled and bustled around the floor, noiselessly and patiently. They knew the problems had only just begun. If that receptionist who had apparently never heard of race-week was on duty now, she would be finding out the hard way.

There was probably no more Irish name among the gathering than Derry Lynch. But the owner of the label could, in his own words, 'hardly be less Irish'. Mr Lynch is the sales manager of the Queens, a task with responsibilities which multiply dramatically during this second week of March. At first glance, Mr Lynch might have been thought barely up to the challenge – the receding hairline and the look of breeding shone through above his traditional top coat and tails in a manner which suggested an aversion to betting and boozing and a horror of brawling. But first impressions, in this case, were quite misleading. Derry Lynch had climbed the hotel ladder very fast and was still a young man. But he was also a tough cookie, well up to the challenge of over-enthusiastic revellers.

We sat in the main bar which was now getting down to providing the fuel the visitors required. Gone, I remarked, were those enormous, impressive potted palms. 'They are worth £250 each,' explained Mr Lynch, 'that makes £1,000 worth of plants. They take up a lot of room so we wouldn't leave them here this week anyway. But purely in terms of their value, we think it is wise to move them – just as we have removed all the valuable furniture from the public rooms and all the paintings from the walls. The criminal element is naturally attracted to the town this week, and you would not believe the things they have pinched from here in the past. Now, we try not to give them the chance.'

Derry Lynch is a born and bred Cheltonian with an admission to make. 'I have never been to the racecourse in my life, never really been interested. Frankly, the side of it I see during Festival week would put me off anyway. Most Cheltenham people hate the racecourse because of the type of people it brings into the town in March – I know a lot of locals who deliberately book their holidays this week so that they miss it. But that is me speaking as a local resident – as an employee of this hotel I must say the business is good and it is simply up to people like myself to make certain things never get out of hand.'

Easier said than done, I suggested. Derry agreed. 'Ninety-five per cent of our guests this week are Irish. Most of them stay here every March. By Thursday, you can be sure we will be half-full for next year's Festival already. We all know why most of them come – to drink and to gamble. That they choose the Queens as a base is certainly good for trade, but it makes for a difficult week. For instance, I am doing shifts of twenty-four hours on, then twenty-four hours off. By the end of the week I expect to feel absolutely shattered.'

Late each night, the bar of the Queens is one of the great social studies of the sporting calendar ... if you can get in the door. The rich and the poor, the winners and the losers are all there. Racing rules and if, like Lynch, you suffer from claustrophobia, it is not a place to linger in too long. But even the long-suffering sales manager admits: 'The atmosphere is wonderful.'

'People occasionally misbehave. Of course they do. Last year, I made 50p in tips all week because I seemed to do nothing else but throw people out. Mostly, these are not residents but chaps who have come in here to carry on drinking, having made several stops on the way. But the residents are bound by largely the same rules. If they don't toe the line in a reasonable manner, we would throw them out, too.

'We have plain-clothes security men around the hotel this week. Yes, a lot more than usual, but then that goes for the entire staff, which virtually doubles for Festival week. This is an entirely different hotel for one week every year and all of us just have to accept that fact. I can't say I enjoy the week – it is the one part of the job I don't enjoy – but it is a challenge, the sort of thing which gives one a sense of fulfilment when it has been safely and satisfactorily completed.'

The police purge on illegal gambling had made a difference to the Queens. 'I'm told it used to be like Las Vegas here, but during the last two Festivals I can guarantee we were not aware of any gambling going on in the public rooms. If they do it in their own bedrooms, as I suspect they do, there is nothing we are entitled to do or would want to do to stop them. The police do keep a close eye on the place, though, and it is very much our duty to make sure the cards don't come out in the bars or the lounges.'

On a normal Festival night, the shutters will come down on the main bar in the hotel around 2am. If the Irish are in an especially celebratory mood, it might be a little later to allow time for the purchase of a few last bottles of bubbly. But in any event, residents can still send the night porter in search of their fancy. The night porter is much in demand this week. 'There is not normally much drinking going on after about 3.30am,' said Mr Lynch conservatively. He did concede that the staff do occasionally stumble over slumbering bodies when they come down to prepare the breakfast, however. Some of the revellers can't quite remember the way to their rooms.

'When I worked in Southampton, at another good-class hotel, I had a similarly hectic week to cope with, for the Boat Show,' said Derry. 'But it was not quite like this. Mind you, come back on Friday and we will be completely back to normal – the pictures back on the wall, the furniture back in place, even the potted palms returned to the bar. You won't know we have been hit ... and, believe me, we will be hit.'

It was difficult to imagine such scenes of drunkenness and debauchery gracing the bars of the de la Bere Hotel. All the pictures remained in place on the walls there, the public rooms looked as gracefully opulent as ever and the bells had not been removed from the towers in case anyone took a fancy to pinching them. In short, life was going on much as normal but for the fact that every room in the place had been booked out months before at vastly inflated prices, and the hotel stood to make a minor fortune from a week's work.

Not that you would have known it. Shortly after six, when I pulled up on the gravel-covered car park facing this most striking of country houses, there was not exactly a rush on. Outside, the tennis courts and putting green waited silently for summer, and lights illuminated the entrances to the library and the study bar. It is the sort of place Bertie Wooster's Aunt Dahlia must live in, and conveniently on the very edge of the racecourse – clearly visible from the new stand. Yet you would scarcely have known that something special was about to happen at the bottom of the garden by the utter emptiness of the main bar, where two young barmen prowled behind their counter and looked suitably surprised when I disturbed their company and made a crowd of three.

'There'll only be residents in tonight,' one of them said. 'But we'll be busy tomorrow lunch. And as for Thursday ...' he whistled through his teeth at the prospect. 'Last year on Gold Cup lunchtime we took £274 behind this bar. I know that's right because we wrote the figure on the ceiling here,' he added, pointing upwards as if I needed further convincing of his mathematics.

I drank a pint of good beer in splendid surroundings and wondered where all the £660-a-person-four-day-deal guests were lurking. Perhaps they had spent out on the rooms and couldn't afford to venture into the bar.

The only clue that there was racing afoot came with the brief, harassed appearance of a middle-aged guest. Having asked whether my evening paper carried the day's results and been given a negative response, he hastened out of the bar again in search of a radio. He didn't stop for a drink, but his punting had plainly begun. I left at seven, leaving the de la Bere bar quite empty again.

Down in the racecourse office, the frantic activity slowed to a gallop around 6.30. There were plenty of visitors with their problems and their questions. Tim Hamey was among them, collecting tickets for himself and his wife Phyllis and, no doubt, regaling all of those present with a story from half a century ago. Such is the man's character that everyone, no matter how busy, would have spared a few minutes to listen, too.

In Prestbury village, Diana Nicholson had paid the second of her twice-daily visits to Frenchie's nursing-home bedside and was now contemplating the three days ahead. She intended to be present for all the racing but was not convinced it would bring her much pleasure. 'I have hated the Festival in the past,' she admitted. 'Oh, the atmosphere is marvellous and the racing is the best one could see. But years ago, I was always fretting about whether David was going to get on the floor and now, more recently, I have got myself into a state worrying about how his horses will run. It can take all the enjoyment away.'

Edward Gillespie went home to his wife and children, a mere five-minute drive from the course. Philip Arkwright kept to a time-honoured custom and dined with his predecessor, Charlie Toller, before settling into the dubious comfort of his temporary quarters. Phil Hatcher glanced skywards and saw no sign of rain, before stooping to pass through the door of his bungalow at the top of the course. For all of them it would be a fretful night, not one expected to sleep very soundly.

But back at the Queens the first of the week's parties was accelerating nicely. In hotels all around Cheltenham, toasts were drunk to the success of the three days coming. And in houses all over England, jockeys, trainers and owners said their own private prayers for the most important meeting of the year. Few would be fully answered.

Chapter 9

THE COMMOTION WOKE ME at 4.30am. It was a distant din at first and only when it encamped outside my door did my sleepy brain register the facts. Here we had two Irishmen returning from a night of what they do best, only to find that the manager of the admirable Wyastone Hotel had given up his vigil at 3.45am and locked them out. The boys, judging by their strident tones, did not seem to think that this was quite the treatment they merited and felt it wise to announce their views to the rest of the guests, inserting half-a-dozen especially loud expletives just to get the message across to any who did not wake up in time to catch it at once.

Sheikh Ali Abu Khamsin with his Half Free after winning the Mildmay of Flete Challenge Cup at the 1984 Festival. The horse was trained by Fred Winter and ridden by Sheikh Ali's regular jockey Richard Linley.

Their door, which happened to be next to mine, was shut without sensitivity and peace reigned once more.

It was a harmless enough incident, indicative of many such scenes around the town on this and the next two nights, and it did at least ensure that I was fully alert in ample time for the dawn patrol on the racecourse, an event dear to the hearts of many who have been attending the Festival more years than they care to recall. I crept out of my room at 6.30, noticing that alongside the predictable copies of the *Sun* and the *Sporting Life* outside my snoring neighbours' door was a single, discarded boot, either lost in the stumbling mêlée of two hours earlier or left deliberately to adhere to a mysterious County Cork superstition.

The morning was cold and windy, the pavements still damp from an overnight shower, nothing like heavy enough to answer Irish prayers and soften the going in the direction of their more accustomed heavy to boggy. There was hardly a car on the streets in the town, just the occasional milk-cart and a juggernaut heading for the cones and queues of the M5, but the racecourse itself was already alive. Staff had begun to arrive at about the time my hotel manager was locking out his Irish guests, but security officers, both in and out of uniform, had manned the gates and patrolled the grounds all night. The stables, where the most precious of the course's temporary possessions had spent the night, were also under constant surveillance and now the lads had emerged from their hostel in busy, cosily-dressed clusters and were doing their best to pretend that it was just another day.

It wasn't, of course. For the horses who were even now being led out for exercise, for their lads and their connections, it was quite probably the most important day of the year. For the Irish jockeys, several of whom dead-heated with me through the gates, it was also very much more than the regular race-meeting, more even than a potentially rich pay-day. It was the battle with the English which counted as much as anything, perfectly summed up by Edward O'Grady, one of their most successful trainers. 'Our jockeys come over as a team and they like to feel part of that unit,' he said. 'They are riding as individuals, but they also go out at Cheltenham to ride for Ireland.'

O'Grady's two Tuesday runners, Poet's Corner and Mister Donovan, were among the first out on the middle of the course for a gentle pre-race gallop. The tradition is among the most time-honoured of the meeting, although only in recent years has it become popular as a public spectacle. Photographer Bernard Parkin has witnessed these proceedings since the days of Cottage Rake, and recalls: 'There were never any spectators other than those directly connected with the horses. Nowadays, dozens of people come along and see it as being part of their day out.'

There was certainly a healthy gathering of interested watchers huddled together near the helicopter pad, among them the best-known of all Ireland's gamblers, J.P. McManus. A small, dark man with an intelligent and friendly face, McManus's racing interests extend to bookmaking and owning his own horses. But it is for betting with furious certainty and considerable success that he has made his reputation and this morning his arrival from his Festival base in Broadway was taken to be a sign of an Irish good thing at exercise. Most of the back-of-the-hand mutterings among the *cognoscenti* concerned a horse called Nore Prince, who came across the Irish Sea with only one hurdles race, and one impressive win to his name yet was widely fancied to beat vastly more experienced rivals in the first event of the Festival, the Waterford Crystal Supreme Novices Hurdle. His trainer was new to me – one R.J. Whitford who, Philip Arkwright assured me, 'Has been here forever – he and his horses were first to arrive and even that was two days behind their original schedule.'

Philip had spent his usual, restive night and had woken in some alarm at 5am to the sound of raindrops spattering against the white-painted windows of the ambulance room. Although quickly establishing that there was no cause for alarm, he had accepted the impossibility of further sleep, washed and dressed, and was now present on the gallops for the moment that most of the morning crowd had risen early to see. Dawn Run, the Champion Hurdle favourite, applied the prerogative of the high-class female and arrived on the scene later than expected, her progress fussed over at every step by the unmistakeable form of her owner Mrs Charmian Hill.

Dressed in a red-riding-hood jacket, her whispy grey hair lifted protestingly back by the breeze, Mrs Hill looked the sort of old lady who should be doing nothing more strenuous than a little gardening, a little shopping and an after-lunch snooze. Instead, given her own way, she would not only have been present to preside over the final preparations of her horse, she would have ridden the animal herself.

Mrs Hill, perhaps more than anyone else at the meeting, epitomised the National Hunt habit, and the Cheltenham obsession, for placing spirit above logic. At sixty-five years old, with a figure which suggested that a gust of wind off the Cotswolds might do her some permanent damage, she was still regularly riding horses and would have continued to compete under the rules of racing but for the authorities' decision to refuse her a licence on the grounds of her own safety. At the time she was a mere sixty-three and had just partnered her beloved Dawn Run to a flat-race victory at Tralee so she felt justified in contesting the decision. But to no avail. The doctor's wife from Waterford, whose amiable husband resigns himself to her predilection with no more than a shrug and a smile, was forced to nominate another jockey for Dawn Run. And thereby hangs another tale.

Cheltenham history is littered with stories of aggrieved jockeys. No better example springs to mind than Tommy Kinane, who partnered Monksfield to win the 1978 version of the Champion Hurdle and was then 'jocked off' in favour of Dessie Hughes the following March. Many racegoers found it an unforgiveable act, no matter that Hughes won, and poor, little Tommy's fate was to be quickly forgotten by all but his closest friends and most faithful supporters.

In the Dawn Run story there was no such publicised episode, simply a long-running backstage rumour which refused to go away. The facts were these: when the horse won at Aintree in 1983, and then came out to give Gaye Brief such an almighty scare the following day, her partner was Tony Mullins, the young son of the restrained, reclusive trainer, Paddy Mullins. It was widely assumed in Ireland that Mullins junior would keep the ride, and keep the horse in the family, in the build-up to a tilt at Cheltenham but, apparently on the insistence of Mrs Hill and no doubt to the mixed and confused reaction of Mullins senior, Jonjo O'Neill was recruited to fly over from England whenever Dawn Run was engaged. He was, however, not put under contract and it was close to Festival time before he was categorically assured he would have the Champion Hurdle ride. The saga was to have a twist in the tail, as Tony Mullins regained the coveted partnership for Aintree and Auteuil due to an O'Neill injury and his father, more vocal than usual, confided to the media that he thought the horse improved by several lengths for his son's handling.

This, however, was all in the future as Mrs Hill, interviewed on the gallops by television's maestro of a commentator, Peter O'Sullevan, expressed her regrets that the going was not softer, her wish that the horse should be ridden up with the pace and her confidence that, within a few hours, she would have something to celebrate.

By eight o'clock, the exercise ceremony was reaching its climax, anxious trainers casting final, fretful eyes over their meal-tickets as they stretched their limbs in a lazy, private preview of what was to come.

Phil Hatcher had been on the course before five o'clock. Sheer force of habit, he admitted to himself, because the job was surely done. But, as ever on the first morning of the meeting, the foreman was anything but idle. 'There never seems to be much to do when you get out there, but there is always plenty once you start,' he said as he cossetted an enormous mug of coffee in the club office. Betty, her eyes alive like a child's on Christmas morning, had arrived at her desk at 8am and found the switchboard lights already flashing with calls from the absent-minded, the pedantic and the panicking. She was rude to no-one, which in itself represented an achievement at such an ungodly hour, but neither did she encourage lengthy conversations. There was far too much to do to indulge in idle chatter on this of all days. Secretary Rosemary Hammond came in for a brief but productive couple of hours at her usual office desk before taking up her position at the enquiries counter in the members' lobby. 'The last week has been very hectic,' she reported, 'but we have hardly started yet. I have to be prepared for virtually anything today. It is the only attitude if we are to cope.'

Shortly after 8.30 the main entrance to the course resembled a factory at clocking-on time, with a stream of staff bearing handbags, umbrellas and lunch-packs filing in for their day's work. They wore the blank look of the uninvolved and the unexcited to distinguish themselves from the animated expressions which would belong to the arriving racegoers in just a few hours time. All around Cheltenham at that moment, hangovers were being tackled with painkillers of porridge, codis and coffee, and on hundreds of breakfast tables the diners were obscured behind their *Sporting Lifes*, the formlines and the betting forecasts being studied with furrowed brows and vivid determination.

Nothing changes. The scene would have been much the same thirty-nine years earlier when, with the end of the war imminent and racing gearing up for a full-scale resumption, a Welshman named Davy Jones won the Cheltenham Gold Cup aboard Red Rower. It was not one of the most powerful Gold Cup fields, the calls of the services had made certain of that, but it was a notable win in a number of ways. Red Rower was owned and trained by Lord Stalbridge, the only man to prepare his own horse for Gold Cup triumph, and the winning time appears in the race's annals as a track record – a misleading statistic as a section of the course had been taken for agricultural needs during the war and the race was a quarter-mile shorter than usual. No, it was the jockey who made this one of Cheltenham's romantic triumphs.

Davy Jones began his apprenticeship in Prestbury, under trainer Ben Roberts, in 1925 but had to wait until he was thirty-seven before landing the greatest prize of all. Most jockeys would have settled for that and slipped happily into retirement, immortalised by the victory. But not Davy. Three years after winning on Red Rower he did actually give up jump racing ... and turned instead to riding on the flat. He was just forty when he took up his new career, and he might still be riding today if he had not suffered the same fate as Mrs Charmian Hill and been grounded by the stewards. In Davy's case, however, it was the Nairobi stewards who told him their view that a sixty-five-year-old should really be seeking gentler pursuits. For twenty-five years he had ridden wherever his fancy and his reputation took him, and that included India, Denmark, the Far East and America. He says he intended to retire some years earlier and had actually visited Kenya only for a holiday. 'The people there persuaded me to take out my licence again,' he grins. And when the stewards finally pensioned him off, he still wasn't finished. The indomitable Davy set up an academy for prospective African apprentices, which kept him occupied for a few more months until he terminated his travels and returned to England. His working life ended with a spell as assistant to trainer David Robinson before he retired, a good bit later than planned, and came back to live in Cheltenham, the place where it all began more than half-a-century earlier.

Like his great friend and contemporary Tim Hamey, Davy Jones was not in the habit of missing Cheltenham meetings and he would be there for the Champion Hurdle, following his well-worn path between the weighing-room, where he knew everyone, and his customary perch on the steps outside the Mandarin Bar, where he would regale anyone who cared to listen with a selection of his experiences. Just a face in the vast crowd, but a face containing an endless series of racing memories.

In the early sixties, when Davy Jones was still engaged on his world tour, the Cotswold Hotel in Portland Street was one of Cheltenham's more nondescript pubs – a tiny, cramped two-bar inn of the type that looks run-down from the outside and does not dispel the impression the other side of the door. But then Conn Carroll arrived, and everything changed. Today, every Irishman who comes to Cheltenham knows the Cotswold and, during Festival week, most of them are in the pub at least once each day.

Even the directors of the Steeplechase Company regularly patronise Mr Carroll's establishment, and it has become the accepted venue for the annual Friday lunchtime official inquest on every Festival.

It was sardine-packed before midday as the Champion Hurdle pro-gramme fast approached. Conn, born in County Cork of a family with equine leanings that meant he could ride almost before he could walk, presided behind the long, single bar with which he had transformed the pub when he took it on 'after ten years in London, warming up.' A large, amiable man with steel-rimmed glasses, smart suits and a permanent smile, he was carving from one of the thirty joints of prime beef he expected to see consumed over the three days. He was now an old hand at the Cheltenham race game and he knew exactly how much of his spectacularly good food to order, how much beer and champagne to store in his cellar and, most important of all, how to retain the atmo-sphere which attracted the punters like a magnet – and not only from Ireland.

Conspicuous by a check coat as loud as his Eastern States drawl, a customer named Larry polished off an enormous plate of beef and announced himself satisfied. 'This,' he said, 'is the best pub in England.

I would come over just to visit here again, never mind the racing.' It transpired that Larry had been to Cheltenham every Festival for twenty years until contracting cancer. He had survived it for five years, he said, and his doctors had told him that this was to be his last trip to England. 'I'm going back to be buried,' he boomed, writing himself off in such a cheerful manner that I hardly knew whether to sympathise or share his joke.

Larry, of course, had stories to tell. He had once come over for the meeting aboard the *Queen Mary*, celebrated rather too vigorously and had been about to embark for the return journey when he was gently told he was getting on the wrong ship. He had been present at Aintree for the remarkable Grand National victory by Jay Trump and dedicated American Tommy Smith. Having pulled off a substantial gamble on the horse, Larry was directed back to his hotel by the helpful British beat bobbies and remembers distributing £5 notes 'for the boys to have a decent dinner'. Only two days later, he discovered that what he had been handing out was in fact £50 notes. He cared not a jot. If money had not often been much object to Larry, then fun most certainly came easily to him, and if this was genuinely to be his final Cheltenham, he deserved to have a good one.

I left genial Conn reminiscing about the trophies he had had to fill in the past for dizzily successful owners; the Gold Cup itself had apparently been swamped in champagne in the Cotswold bar before now. The landlord looked forward to hosting plenty of happy parties in the days ahead and, as soon as he could close the door on the last lunchtime customer, he intended to hurry up the hill himself to see the action.

Back in the roaring 'twenties, when membership of Boodles, the Reform or the Naval and Military Club ensured a smooth passage into Cheltenham, the one problem a chap had at the course was that he could never find a seat.

True, the annual subscription was only five pounds sixteen shillings, which did include entertainments tax and did get one into eight days' racing. One could also bring in three chums, providing they were the right types, as one did not wish to be blackballed when the committee next met. But it *was* infernally hard finding a seat.

The club handbook stated, quite categorically, that 'seats in the drawing-room or verandah cannot be reserved'. So where did that leave one? The club had thought of that. 'The same rule applies to the lawn seats, but in order to meet the wishes of those members who desire to secure private seats, the Committee have sanctioned the hire of seats, provided that the names or initials of members are painted on them, and also that the Committee reserve the right to arrange the positions.' Hence, the park benches which, even now, sit in front of the lower members' enclosures bearing names of members. In the twenties, they could be hired for one guinea a year, in the open, or three guineas for the luxury of staying under cover, and woe betide anyone whose backside was placed on someone else's property. The current cost is £15 per year and Phil Hatcher considers it one of his most important tasks for the early October meeting to ensure the benches are in the correct order.

Things have changed a bit since then. Cries of complaint can still regularly be heard from leg-weary racegoers at the March meeting but, for those willing to pay for the privilege, seats are not in such short supply. Any of Cheltenham's two thousand annual members could apply for comfortable reserved seats high up in the new grandstand, a five-level luxury development, which was to have its latest extension opened by Lord Willoughby de Broke before the first race of the 1984 Festival.

The extension, built in just eleven months to a schedule that must be the envy of many planners and many more frustrated buyers, catered not only for the members but also that coveted and cosseted new breed, the sponsors and private boxholders. Thirteen new boxes, each seating twelve people for lunch and including a balcony, were built and priced at £4,500 a year. Not only were they immediately let, there was also a seventeen-year waiting list for their use.

If some rue such progress, others revel in it, especially the executives escaping from their office for a free and pampered day at the races in one of the twenty-nine viewing boxes and sixteen lunch rooms which now stretch along the upper levels of the impressively space-age facilities.

Edward Gillespie hoped that few people would even notice the changes. It wasn't that he was ashamed of them, rather that the project would be deemed a success so long as not too many hankered after the past. The basic principle employed in all the racecourse's developments has been to take the entertainment to the customer rather than expect him to go on an expedition to find it – for example, the concourses which now link the stands with the new parade ring, where terracing provides viewing space for over four thousand in a paddock development which cost around £2 million. Some, naturally, moaned that the atmosphere of the place had gone. Gillespie sighs. 'The winners' enclosure was in the same position for seventeen years. People got used to it, and it was marvellous for the five hundred who could witness the unsaddling – but very frustrating for the other four thousand who would have liked to!'

So Cheltenham was expanded, modernised or ruined, depending on your standpoint. The stands which had lasted for well over half a century were gradually disappearing and soon, perhaps in another fifteen years, they may have disappeared altogether. Not everyone would be pleased ... but most would find life more comfortable.

*Champion amateur rider Dermot Browne's first visit to the Cheltenham
winner's enclosure was in 1978 when Mr Kildare, trained by his father Liam,
won the Sun Alliance Novices' Hurdle. Mr Kildare never went anywhere
without the family pony Billy Boy and he was there in the winner's enclosure
to greet Mr Kildare. In charge of Billy Boy – on whom all the Browne children
learned to ride – is Dermot.*

The new Festival began just as the last one had ended, with triumph for
Michael Dickinson. The tanned and fretful figure of the young maestro
of Harewood once again stood, relieved, in the winner's enclosure after
his young amateur Dermot Browne had brought home his own horse
Browne's Gazette in the Waterford Crystal Supreme Novices Hurdle and
foiled the first big gamble of the meeting, on the locally-trained Townley
Stone. Rather than slapping Mr Browne on the back and joining in the
general revelries, however, stickler Dickinson issued a stern rebuke. Some
yards before the line, Browne had allowed the great moment to get the
better of him and raised his fist in a gesture of unrestrained delight. 'It

was stupid,' said the trainer. 'He can do that sort of thing when the horse has won if he likes, but not before the line.'

But Browne had started a trend. Although his horse was trained in Yorkshire, he himself was very Irish. The invaders claimed 'Gazette as their first victory and then crowed immodestly when Bobsline won an epic battle with Noddy's Ryde for the Arkle Trophy. As John Karter wrote in the following day's *Times*, 'It is daunting enough for the English when the Irish have any sort of winner at Cheltenham. But when, as happened with Bobsline, that winner is the long-time Irish banker bet at the meeting you wonder whether it is prudent to be heard with an English accent as you become slowly submerged by the relentless tide of whooping, fist-waving visitors. It is all good-natured stuff, though. Many Irishmen slave and save for the entire year with just one aim – to pile the lot on their crack horses at the Festival – so who can begrudge them their unfettered festivity?'

Certainly, Jonjo O'Neill would not, as he sat in the weighing-room, sipped a half-cup of tea and waited with the familiar expectancy teasing his muscles as the Waterford Crystal Champion Hurdle drew near, the moment when he hoped, and almost everyone else expected he would rubber-stamp Ireland's domination of early proceedings with victory on Dawn Run.

Jonjo had won the hurdling crown before – on Sea Pigeon in 1980, and would have won it again the following March but for an injury which presented the mount to his greatest rival John Francome. Now here he was aboard the odds-on favourite, riding as much for his native Ireland as for himself.

He was born in Fermoy, County Cork, shortly after the 1952 Gold Cup. His three brothers had no interest in horses but Jonjo's father encouraged his fascination for racing and, after many moments of self-doubt and a false start or two, the name of J. J. O'Neill was launched on the British racing public. As a breed, they were to come to love the little curly-haired imp whose face seems forever wreathed in smiles. As a man, he was to come to love Cheltenham.

'Where I come from, the Festival is a constant talking-point,' he explains. 'It is *the* place to go, an obsession for many owners and trainers. They want a winner at Cheltenham and the whole season is aimed at getting it. When I was young I used to watch my heroes, Tommy Carberry and Pat Taaffe, ride at the course and dream that one day I might get there to watch it in person. I never dared to believe I might ride there.'

O'Neill exceeded his dreams, but slowly. He came to the Festival for the first time in 1972, when an apprentice with Cumbrian trainer Gordon Richards, and led up their Gold Cup runner Titus Oates. Later the

Dawn Run leads Desert Orchid on the first circuit of the 1984 Champion Hurdle.

same year he was back, this time to ride in the Mackeson Gold Cup. It was only his fourth ride over fences and, typically telling the story against himself, he relates: 'I came to the last with every chance of winning, went for a big one and jumped myself clean out of the saddle. I was on my backside, feeling pretty foolish, when the winner passed the post.'

The highs and lows since that day are well documented, as are the mental anguish and physical torture he suffered following the appallingly bad break of his right leg at Bangor. But Jonjo is nothing if not tough, and as he walked out of the plush new weighing-room, acknowledged the inevitable well-wishers, grinned at a friend or two and headed for the paddock in the red and black colours of Ireland's favourite mare, he would not have swapped jobs with anyone in the world.

All went to plan early on. Desert Orchid, the well-backed young novice, set a strong gallop and Jonjo had the favourite tucked in behind. At the top of the hill, the grey pacemaker dropped out of contention and Dawn Run took it up. One potential challenger after another made a run for the front only to be effortlessly beaten off, but as they turned into the straight with O'Neill's black cap plainly visible in the lead, out of the chasing pack came the blue and gold of a 66-1 outsider, Cima, ridden by the long-suffering Peter Scudamore. At the last flight Dawn Run's lead had shrunk alarmingly and as two of Britain's finest jockeys got down to work on their mounts, half the crowd of 25,516 held its breath while the

The amazing scene in the winner's enclosure after Dawn Run's victory.

other roared its lungs to distraction. It was a memorable duel, but Cima and Scudamore never quite got up, the three-quarters of a length verdict going the way of Dawn Run and leaving Scudamore still wondering where his first Festival winner would come from.

The Irish quickly dismissed the fact that their pride and joy had very nearly been upstaged by an apparent no-hoper. They gathered noisily in their hundreds at the entrance to the unsaddling enclosure, sweeping in behind their heroes as if the police and security men had never even bothered to turn up. No-one minded. Even Miles Gosling, chairman of the Steeplechase Company, said indulgently: 'This is their hour and you cannot blame them. This is what they came over to see.'

For the next ten minutes, pandemonium reigned. O'Neill, grinning as even he had never done before, was lifted off the horse and engulfed. Mrs Hill was thrown high into the air by hysterical supporters and came up smiling stronger than ever, as if to prove she was perfectly sturdy enough to have ridden the horse herself. But Paddy Mullins, who had prepared the horse for triumph in his yard at Goresbridge, County Kilkenny, lived up to his retiring reputation by slipping away from the scene of celebrations and leaving it to owner and rider to express themselves to the waiting press.

Winning at Cheltenham, you see, takes different people in different ways. Some want to shout, some want to cry, others just want to be alone with their thoughts.

Losers are traditionally forgotten, and Peter Scudamore knew it. He felt a shade hard done by, for O'Neill's mount had hung badly to the right on the straight and there had looked to be good grounds for a stewards' enquiry. But he took one swift look at the temperature of the Irish ecstasy and decided it would be unwise to object. The stewards had in any case had a very good view of what went on and did not consider that any infringement of the rules had taken place. With what was by now becoming habitual resignation, he accepted yet another second-place and changed into the famous royal blue colours of Lord Vestey's Gold-spun. Cheltenham's sporting peer was not expecting *his* first Festival win here, but Scudamore produced his difficult ride to such perfection after the last flight of the Stayers' Hurdle that it seemed all their ambitions – Vestey's, Scudamore's and David Nicholson's – were to be realised at once. Instead, Mercy Rimell's Gaye Chance stormed through to win by a length and a half. The saga continued. Second again.

The fifth race on the first-day card is the Kim Muir Memorial Challenge Cup. This was to be the thirty-ninth running, which gave a clue to the reason for the memorial. Kim Muir was only twenty-three when he died, killed in action during the war – stunting a highly promising career of an amateur rider who lived near Cheltenham, at Postlip Hall. Originally worth £1,000 and restricted to officers of HM Forces, the Kim Muir still survives as an amateur riders' race, now worth £10,000, and in 1984 it was fittingly won by a Cheltenham-based jockey of the modern era, the immensely popular Jim Wilson.

By comparison with this relatively young event, the final race is an antique. The Grand Annual Chase dates back one hundred and fifty years and its earliest winners included a horse called Lottery, who subsequently won Aintree's first Grand National, and a jockey called Captain Becher, who lent his name to the most famous of Liverpool obstacles. It would be fair to say the race is among the lesser lights of the glittering Festival card now, but punters love it. In recent years, it has been won almost exclusively by first or second favourites, and it happened again, O'Neill recovering his composure after the emotional buffeting he received following Dawn Run's win and completing a 'double' aboard Mossy Moore.

The punters left, reluctantly. It takes a fair while to clear twenty-five thousand people out of a racecourse even when they are all keen to go.

The 1984 Kim Muir Memorial Challenge Cup was won by the well-known local amateur Jim Wilson on Broomy Bank (centre).

When the last thing on their mind is going home, when the solace of sorrow-drowning or the unconfined delight of a few winners persuades them to return to the bars for a final bottle, afternoon becomes evening and evening almost night before the festive lunacy which is afoot all week here abates for a few hours, and peace reigns over Prestbury.

As always on such occasions, there were those who made fools of themselves, some more amenably than others. As always, the office staff uncomplainingly accepted their role as target for much of the mischief and abuse. Louise Gold, press officer of the Racing Information Bureau, seemed positively to enjoy it: 'People come up trying to get a free badge by pretending they are someone else, attached to a certain newspaper. But when I know the person concerned, and know he has already got his badge, it's a game only I can win.'

Secretary Rosemary Hammond could also look back and laugh. Her traumas had included a man whose coat had been stolen, a group who complained that their seats in the temporary grandstand were akin to sitting in a tent in the middle of a field, and another man angry that his lunch guests had not met him. In all three cases, the customer illogically put the blame for everything onto the shoulders of Mrs Hammond and did not get the response he expected. 'I agree with everyone,' she explains. 'They normally go away either thinking I'm mad or wholly self-satisfied at what they believe to be a triumph.'

Wednesday at Cheltenham is traditionally the Queen Mother's day or as it is affectionately called 'Queen Mum's Day'. Her own day, her own race. And, being everybody's idea of the perfect grandmother, the lady is welcomed and feted and nobody would have it any different. Even the police.

The fact is, however, that the Queen Mother's excursions to Cheltenham – and she normally comes on at least two of the three March racing days – present a teasing equation to the two hundred uniformed police officers and innumerable plain-clothes detectives who patrol the course.

One has only to wander into Prestbury village on Gold Cup morning to see why the dearest, fluffiest and best-loved member of our royal family is at once the delight of the public and the despair of the police force. Every year, she follows the same routine, directing her chauffeur to divert from the route to the course in order to stop off at her favourite confectioner, where she receives a bag of her favourite sweets and chats animatedly to the highly-honoured proprietors. Naturally enough, the housewives and children of the vicinity vote unanimously to attend and, naturally enough, the police fear is that a mischief-maker or worse may infiltrate the happy throng. So they erect yellow crash barriers and a security blanket as foolproof as can be managed while adhering to the Queen Mother's insistence that no uniformed policemen accompany her.

The major event on the Wednesday card is the Queen Mother Champion Chase and the patron saint of jump racing is, of course, on hand to present the prizes. This is another sensitive time for the security-conscious and in 1983, horror of horrors, a man broke into the unsaddling enclosure during the ceremony and shook hands with the Queen Mother. Nothing more – he just shook hands and vanished once again into the crowd. But this was quite enough to cause a flutter of panic in the force, enough to make sure that they would be on the lookout for anyone trying something similar the next year. What they did not expect was to catch the original culprit going for the double.

Superintendent Joe Skipsey saw it as a challenge, just as he viewed the entire week. He had been stationed at Cheltenham for only five months

HM Queen Elizabeth the Queen Mother is a regular and popular visitor at the National Hunt Festival.

and this was his first experience of the Festival, though he was no stranger to major sporting events and their peculiar problems. Back in Newcastle, where his accent revealed he felt at home, the superintendent had often been in charge of a four hundred-strong force policing the same size soccer crowd as Cheltenham drew. Same size, different mentality – as he quickly pointed out. One day into the Festival, Superintendent Skipsey reported that the operation was not as bad as he had been led to believe.

It was a well-rehearsed routine. Police leave had been cancelled in several neighbouring areas in order that the local force could be brought up to the required strength, and the superintendent had personally briefed everyone on their duties on the opening morning. Despite the size of the Tuesday crowd – five hundred and twenty-six up on the previous year's corresponding day and three thousand up on 1982 – both the number of offences and their level in the criminal pecking order gave the police cause for self-congratulation. There were only two arrests, and by the following morning just two minor pickpocketing incidents were unresolved.

Tuesday night's revelries in the town centre might be thought to have stretched police resources from the evidence of a one hundred per cent increase in positive breathalyser tests. But a closer inspection reveals that the figure rose from one to two, and that the only other driver tested gave a negative sample.

Joe Skipsey does not bother about drunks on the racecourse, so long as they don't inflict their condition on others. 'It is private property,' he explains. 'People should be encouraged to enjoy themselves, and if that means singing and dancing, we are quite happy to see it.' To prove it, he had prefaced the statement with an indulgent smile at a middle-aged man whose steering seemed to have failed him as he made his way to the racecourse exit.

Pickpockets, however, are an altogether different matter, a breed on whom the police are always eager to wage war. But, mingling with the determination to rid public gatherings of what is certainly a social menace, there lurks a suspicion of admiration for the skill of the pickpocketing teams who roam such places as Cheltenham and who follow the year's sporting diary as rigidly as any budding socialite. The superintendent and his team were stymied by sleight of hand on the opening day, despite making an arrest while the thief's hand was still hovering over the victim's empty pocket. 'The man we arrested did not have the wallet, yet the robbery had undoubtedly taken place because the other man insisted it had gone. So we led everyone up towards the police office at the top of the course, and by the time we got there, the wallet had miraculously reappeared in the pocket of the man who had been robbed. We can only assume that our suspect slipped it immediately to an accomplice, who then saw what had happened to his mate and stealthily returned it as we left the scene of the incident. I have to admit it was clever, and we had no option but to let the man go free because officially no crime had been committed.'

The criminal element who are drawn as if by magnet to Cheltenham in March are not obliging enough to confine their activities to the surrounds of the racecourse. The crowds might be thicker there, providing better camouflage, but late at night in the town's bars and hotels, racegoers have reached a mellow stage and defences are often so far down that they don't even feel the pain of the sting. Like the swank who parked his Rolls-Royce outside the Queens on Tuesday night and returned after a good dinner to find the car present, but his £4,500 radio phone absent.

But on Wednesday, Queen Mum's day, Joe Skipsey and his men enjoyed their finest hour of the week. The operations of security to protect the Queen Mother from further interlopers were deep and discreet, taking in detectives and racecourse staff in addition to uniformed police. So when, at around the time Badsworth Boy was being triumphantly led back after winning the lady's own race for the second successive year, the very same prankster who shook Her Majesty's hand twelve months earlier was spotted advancing for a repeat performance, it needed only a nod and a word on the walkie-talkie before arms were placed on his shoulder and the game was up. Edward Gillespie, modest to the end, admitted that he made an erroneous interjection to the proceedings by grabbing the wrong man, but the culprit was safely collared and led away to explain himself, while the Queen Mother continued to beam in happy oblivion at all and sundry.

It turned out that the phantom hand-shaker was just one of those chaps who can't resist a dare. Having successfully accomplished his hazardous mission the previous year, he had taken a bet that he could do exactly the same thing again, and paid the price. But, like the pickpocket being saved by his accomplice's skill, he had not actually committed an offence to warrant a charge. Joe Skipsey reported that a strong warning had been issued and, in his native Geordie tongue, wryly assessed that he was unlikely to try anything similar again.

Cheltenham's prizes are so rich and the occasion so great that it is by no means rare for a horse to run twice over the course of the three-day Festival, but I doubt if any animal has equalled the achievement of The Freshman in 1861, when he won the Grand Annual Chase and the National Hunt Chase on the same day. As the National Hunt event was over four miles, this seems no mean feat but it is worth qualifying. For one thing, even the best of steeplechase races of that generation were run at what now seems no more than hunting pace. For another, the owner of the victorious horse, who would now pick up more than £20,000 for such an astonishing double, collected a mere fraction of that. The prize for this first-ever running of the National Hunt Chase was just £150.

The race survives today. Along with the Grand Annual, it is the antiquity of the Festival meeting, and if the course now conforms to convenience rather than tradition it has a faithful following and a peculiar atmosphere to befit a contest of such history.

It has not always been run at Cheltenham, however, and even in that initial year of 1861 it had its problems. The line of the race had to be changed when a Mr John Newman, a farmer through whose land it was due to pass, demanded a payment of £100. Not surprisingly, considering that this represented two-thirds of the prize money, the organisers demurred.

Quaintly, a second National Hunt Chase was run only a week after the Cheltenham race. It took place on a course at Market Harborough in Leicestershire but was regarded by the *cognoscenti* as being very much inferior to the Cheltenham production. 'Welshers,' one scribe of the day re-

ported, 'were much in evidence and carried away a good deal of money ...'
The bounders.

Over the next forty years, the National Hunt Chase was up for grabs, staged by the highest bidder among the suburban courses. In 1904 it returned to Cheltenham and was run at Prestbury Park for two seasons, but Warwick then took over for another five years before, in 1911, it finally found its permanent home. The race, for maiden horses and amateur riders, was, until recently, run over four miles of open country, with no fence jumped twice. To facilitate this, a special course was laid out at Cheltenham in March of 1904, a course which took the runners off the racetrack behind an orchard, through the car park and past the stables, reappearing on the course proper to the right of the stands. There were twenty-four obstacles, some of which were almost five feet in height, and the water jump was reputed to be twelve feet deep.

The National Hunt Chase, which has always attracted big fields, is one of the most gruelling tests of stamina in the jumping season – even now that it is run entirely on the same course and over the same obstacles as the other chases – and for many years it has been unofficially labelled 'the amateurs' Grand National'. In 1950, the *Daily Express* racing correspondent Clive Graham wrote: 'The scene on National Hunt Day is very much a part of a fading England. A bustle of wives and mothers and girlfriends surround the riders in the paddock. The paddock rails are thronged with tweed-clad critics ... there is an agreeable atmosphere of "the sport's the thing" which is part of Cheltenham's charm. The rush to cheer the winner as he comes back to the unsaddling enclosure is evoked by a sincere and genuine sentiment quite unconnected with pecuniary gain.'

That might be an exaggeration, these days. The race may still attract a more corinthian outlook than most other Festival events, but the money available ensures that the leading trainers from England and Ireland are not blind to the possibilities of laying out a horse especially for the race. This was the case in 1984 and, as usual, there was a story attached to the race.

Paddy Mullins, not satisfied with training the winner of the Champion Hurdle, expected to win the National Hunt too. He had a horse called Macks Friendly and on the Tuesday, hours before Dawn Run went out to secure her niche in racing history, Paddy set about finding a new owner for the horse in time for Wednesday's race. He phoned John Mulhearn, an old friend, and was greeted by the reply: 'How can you ask me to buy a horse today? It's the thirteenth. Phone me again tomorrow.' So Paddy phoned again on the Wednesday morning, Mulhearn agreed a price and Macks Friendly became the best day's business he had ever done when he strode up the hill to win unchallenged.

'Dodger' had not had a bet on Macks Friendly. At least, if he had he was not letting on about it. Five hours after the typically exuberant Irish welcome for the winner, and Paddy Mullins' second silent, satisfied with-drawal from the hysteria in the space of twenty-four hours, 'Dodger' leaned meditatively on the reception desk in the lobby of the Queens Hotel and complained that the day's racing had been 'one of the most difficult cards I've ever seen'.

The man known to everyone in jump racing as 'Dodger' is, more properly, Simon McCartney. He is also a professional punter, one of the ever-decreasing number in a trade which requires a touch of bravery, an unfailing memory for the endless essentials in the small-print of the formbook, and innumerable stable contacts whose information and in-tegrity can be trusted. There is nothing illegal, nor even shady, in the business of the full-time gambler, but by the very nature of his battle to beat the bookies he is in a more precarious job than the average deep-sea diver. For 'Dodger', however, it is very definitely a labour of love. Although living in the relative wilderness of the Welsh borders, he travels the country throughout the ten months of the jumping season, never missing a race-day except on the rare occasions when the southernmost meeting might be Perth or Hexham, and spending his 'leisure' hours poring avidly over the formbooks until he can virtually recite them by heart.

'Dodger' is an instantly recognisable figure, whether striding towards the weighing-room in search of information, clad in an enormous khaki-coloured coat which perfectly sets off his comedian's face, or perched on an orange box during a race, binoculars clamped to his eyes long enough to assess accurately progress before shouting down a 'bet in running' to one of the bookies with whom he does business. Everyone likes 'Dodger' and many respect him for his knowledge. Some of the jockeys reckon he tells them when they are going to ride a winner, rather than vice-versa.

Tonight, he was in his element. Cheltenham is a magical place to 'Dodger', as much as it is to any trainer or jockey. No hard-headed gambler, this man – he never wants to divorce himself from the roman-ticism of the sport, much as he enjoys profitting by the business end of it.

He began gambling young, starting out at local greyhound tracks. 'I still go to the dogs occasionally now, just for something to do. I very seldom go flat racing, though. It bores me – they come out of the stalls and it's all over. You can't have a bet in running on a five-furlong race, can you?' He had so far dug deep for a big punt only once during the Festival, a successful touch on Dawn Run, but now, smart in his grey suit and sharp-eyed for acquaintances and pretty girls, he was indulging himself in the social scene he loves almost as much as the racing itself.

'I've been coming to Cheltenham ever since I can remember. I love it, even if I know each year it won't provide many decent bets. I stay in the town, enjoy the racing and then do all the night-spots – the Queens, the wine-bars, the night-clubs. There's always someone interesting about.

'In the old days it was impossible to get in the door of the bar here. Really crazy. I can't understand why the Irish blokes pay extortionate prices for rooms when they never use them. Many is the time I've left here at 2.30am and returned just after breakfast to find the same blokes staggering around with a drink in their hand who were in the bar when I went home. What do they need a room for?'

'Dodger' would be at the course early on Gold Cup morning. Like every professional punter worth the title, he had his homework to do, important conversations to conduct. He would have colleagues or rivals, call them what you will, but I doubt if any will ever have the charisma of Mr McCartney.

Chapter 10

EIGHT HOURS BEFORE THE off, it looked for all the world as if the Cheltenham Gold Cup would be run in a rubbish tip. It was a cold, bleak morning of the type on which dawn must think twice before breaking; the slate-grey sky looked full of snow and the Cheltenham members' lawn looked full of debris. The crowds would begin to stream into the course in a little over three hours and it was difficult to conceive how they could fail to be greeted by a shambles.

The park bench seats which have stood on the lawn through so many generations were strewn symbolically with the relics of yesterday's parties and the evidence of this morning's hangovers. In front of the Mandarin bar, a sparkling white seat with Mrs Isobel Smith's name on the back had done especially well with four empty champagne bottles lying on it and a couple of Guinness empties underneath. Even here, the social standings remained intact.

Discarded racecards, betting tickets and cigarette packets crazily decorated the grass and tarmac. It would not matter if there was a litter

Former royal jockey and now best-selling author Dick Francis starts the Stable Lads' Cross Country Race on the last day of the Festival Meeting, 1984.

142

bin to each square yard, there would still be those who thoughtlessly dropped their rubbish on the ground for somebody else to clear up. At Cheltenham, that somebody drove smartly into the course at 8am to meet his army.

Tim Spencer-Cox says his epitaph will be: 'He spent twenty-five years collecting rubbish.' But as he has already been doing duty for that long at Cheltenham, this might soon have to be adjusted. An educated man with the firm, authoritarian manner essential to his command of one hundred men and women, he disembarked from the blue Land Rover in which he does his tours of inspection and immediately set about delegating. No time can be wasted and, literally, no stone left unturned if the course is to be returned to the immaculate condition every punter and party-goer will expect when they come through the gates sometime before lunch.

With the practised certainty of an experienced campaigner, Mr Spencer-Cox sent out his troops. A ragtag group they looked, too, dressed mostly in jeans, sweaters and woollen hats as they fanned out around the course armed with brooms, black plastic bags and ill-disguised admiration for a girl in their midst, distinctive in tight pink trousers. They were of all ages and, apparently, all backgrounds. The unemployed are, naturally, drawn upon for a week of backbending in the fresh Cotswold air, but Mr Spencer-Cox revealed that his employees include company executives with a yearning for temporary escapism, bakers, butchers and quite a number of holidaying office-workers from the currently controversial GCHQ, just up the road.

Tim Spencer-Cox, dapper in flat cap, anorak and tie, is a builder by trade. 'Twenty-five years ago my company built the car parks on the course. It was then that they asked me if I would take responsibility for clearing up the rubbish. I can't remember why I agreed.' He says he doesn't enjoy the week, seeing it purely as a challenging task and a time-consuming interruption to his regular business activities, but I was not so sure. When he spoke of the job there was an enthusiasm in his voice not entirely consistent with one viewing the operation in clinical, refuse-collecting terms. 'I get up early and do the office mail and paper work before leaving home just before eight,' he explained. 'For the rest of each day I neglect my business. Until five years ago I lived next to the course, which was ideal, but I have a little farther to come now.'

So successful has he been at Cheltenham that Tim now supervises the clearing up at Malvern's Three Counties Show, too. 'And that draws even bigger crowds.' The basic principle, however, remains the same – working against a deadline, beating the crowds.

'Our target, of course, is to finish our job before any of the public arrive. People get to the course earlier on Gold Cup day, which means that we have to work even faster. Starting at 8 o'clock, we have less than three hours to get through. But the deadline gives us an incentive. The most difficult day by far is Friday, when the meeting is over and there is twice as much rubbish to pick up as on any other day. The men are tired and I have to crack the whip now and again to keep them going. Philip Arkwright prays for a dry Thursday, but I pray for a dry Friday, because spending hours in the rain, picking up sodden rubbish by hand – which is the only way it can be done – is a soul-destroying occupation. It can sometimes drive the blokes down towards the tented village, where they think they can hide away and have an easier time. I'm wise to it now, of course, but a few years back we had got to the middle of Friday afternoon when I realised we were a few bodies short. I found them in the marquee, where they had discovered a full barrel of beer and proceeded to empty it. A dozen of them were slumped around the barrel and not in any state to do much more work.'

By the very nature of their business, sifting so many tons of rubbish, the clearing-up corps are bound to find the odd pearl in the rubble. In fact, as one would expect, they find a wide variety of items that their owners would never have deliberately dropped. On Gold Cup day this year they found an Irish driving licence and a winning Tote Double ticket from the previous day. Twelve months earlier, one man picked up a ball of bank-notes which, when unravelled and counted, added up to £100. 'I only ever find two-pence pieces myself,' said Tim, gloomily.

On Wednesday they had found one other unusual item of interest – a naked lady taking a shower in the jockey's changing-room. No questions were asked but you could bet it brightened up the day for a few who might have been finding rubbish-collecting not quite the rest-cure they had been expecting. They got through the job as ever, though, and received the usual, highest compliment, in that few, if any, of the enormous crowd would have given a second thought to how the course had been restored from a shambles to perfection in the matter of a few short hours. 'We don't expect praise,' admits Tim Spencer-Cox. 'If we hear no complaints, then we know the job has been done properly.'

Even before the cleaners moved in, the course was buzzing with activity. Edward Gillespie had arrived at 7.30 and was directing operations from his office, supervising the daily duties and smoothing the threat of more major problems. Philip Arkwright who, of course, had never even left the place, managed to look extraordinarily calm and relaxed as he sat at his desk surrounded by the morning papers, while Phil Hatcher was out on the track directing the removal of plastic railing from old course to new. An aesthetically pleasing routine was taking place in the parade ring, where two of the gardeners were pushing handmowers at right angles to each other, achieving the effect of perfect lines.

The trophies on display, Gold Cup day. The Gold Cup is in the centre and the large trophy on the left is the Christie's Foxhunter Challenge Cup.

Maintenance staff were on duty early. They, too, had suffered their share of panic over the first two days, especially the moment on Wednesday when it was reported that a lift in the new stand had broken down, with twenty-seven people trapped inside. As they are designed to hold about half that number, there was no mystery as to the reason for malfunction.

The gallops were busy again, and among the audience gathering for the exercise of more Irish fancies were three men from across the water who had plainly omitted to spend any time in bed. Unshaven, unkempt and indicating they may have indulged a shade too freely on the giggle-juice, they were having their first row of the day with a taxi-driver over the contentious issue of whether they owed him any money or not. Voices dropped a decibel or two as a police car cruised alongside.

I walked onto the course itself, around the bend and up the long climb towards the winning post. I saw the sight that would, in a few hours time, greet the jockeys on the Tote Gold Cup leaders as they turned into the straight for the final time. The massive stands look remote as the second-last fence looms ahead but you can read the time on the clock high above the silver ring, see the number board below it and, although at this early hour there was only expectant emptiness, the jockeys might even feel the atmosphere of the seething forty thousand crowd as the great race reached its climax.

One thing was certain. To walk the course on this of all days disperses the pain of early rising, excites and stimulates the most hungover mind. And hangovers were plentiful, judging by the scene at my hotel, where the heavy eyes and sensitive expressions suggested that when this week was over, a spell in the rest home, which was handily placed next door, might be in order. It was not surprising. Wednesday is traditionally the night on which hair is let down with a vengeance in preparation for the final day of the meeting, and the scenes on and off the course had supported the impression that there would be many reaching for the dark glasses on Gold Cup morning. Well after 7 pm, when I walked from one end of the stands to the other, there had been no sign of the tempo abating. In the Cottage Rake bar, impromptu singing and dancing had broken out and someone was playing the spoons as accompaniment while others, less energetic, slumped on the floor among the broken glass and betting slips. Bar staff, charged with the desperately difficult duty of clearing up while not interrupting the flow of merriment, tried to negotiate their brooms through the bodies and shift barrels through the debris. Interestingly, the Brown Jack bar at the top, cheap end of the course, was deserted by this hour, the working-class punters having spent out, but as the burger bar served its final customer and the souvenir seller manfully attempted to cajole a few departing figures into a final purchase, the action was merely shifting into the pubs and hotels of Prestbury and Cheltenham. Few are more famous than the Royal Oak in Prestbury village, where some flamboyantly clad folk had gathered for their after-race cocktails. Someone had vomitted in the Gents, but the bar manager remained resolutely cheerful. 'It's the first time this week,' he said, 'and it's a small price to pay for the fun of the races.'

There was a lasting impression from the blatant excesses. Unlike the tribes who follow soccer, drink two cans of cheap lager and try to wreck a train, there was no malicious intent in these revellers. They might wake up with a headache, but I doubted if many would wake up with a black eye or, worse, wake up in jail.

Now that the morning after had arrived, there were more traditions to be observed. Many had followed the same pattern for years, gathering with their friends in the Queens, the Cotswold or the Royal Oak for a pre-noon freshener; some would be at the course before eleven, in order to watch the stable-lads' cross country race; others would be there in the car park with their own food and drink in the boot – tailgating, as they call it in America. But by shortly after 1pm, an hour before the first race on the card, the stands and concourses were packed and the queues for the toilets and the Tote wound back like snakes. The scene was set.

Cheltenham's weighing-room has been moved three times in recent years but it remains basically the same privileged, protected place, guarded by the same keen-eyed men. Commoners can stare from a distance at the warren into which the muddied heroes disappear; owners, trainers and the like can even stand on the terrace outside. But to step through the door without copious accreditation demands either the cunning and stealth of a cat-burglar or a monumental slice of luck.

Ken Pardington is chief doorman and has been for years, as he will tell you with pride. Ken is seventy-eight now and has been coming to Cheltenham since the far-off days when George Duller was the star jockey in the weighing-room. Now, it is Francome, O'Neill and the rest who benefit from the shielding and screening of this superficially stern, but deeply amiable man in the bowler. He wears his 'thou shalt not pass' look with the staunch loyalty of a front-line soldier advancing on the enemy, but engage him in conversation and he is likely to regale you with racing yarns emanating from his native and much-loved Prestbury. Ken is the oldest of the gatemen employed by Pratts for duty at Cheltenham and well aware that, in the eyes of some of the public, he belongs to a breed of 'jobsworths' whose main aim and pleasure in life is to stop people going where they want to go. He has reached the age and experience, however, when this attitude no longer bothers him; he is also, incidentally, not a 'jobsworth' at all but one of the more obliging and co-operative in his trade.

Any interlopers who may get past Mr Pardington will find there is a second line of defence, and a formidable one at that. Bryan Robinson stations himself in the foyer of the weighing-room and very little which goes on around the vicinity of the door escapes his attention, precious few invaders on the hallowed territory escape his strident recriminations. Several times during the March meeting, I observed Mr Robinson bursting through the door like a cork from a bottle to question the presence of individuals or groups who had wandered – mistakenly or otherwise – into the protected area, and those who were not immediately able to present the correct badges were very firmly acquainted with the ground rules for entry to the paddock and weighing-room vicinity. Few, I suspect, would dare to venture back once they have undergone a lecture from the chief of Pratts.

Before racing on Thursday, the weighing-room terraces was more congested than ever and the doormen were at full stretch to keep passages clear and trespassers at bay. Into this hectic scene strode a man who should have worn the excited look of a trainer anticipating a big-race win. Instead, Nicky Henderson looked like a man in the throes of a particularly violent nightmare. Which, in a sense, he was.

Like David Nicholson and Josh Gifford, Henderson was a leading trainer nagged by the knowledge that he had never yet produced a Cheltenham Festival winner. And, just as Nicholson's father is inextricably linked with Cheltenham's past, so Henderson's father is very much a part of Cheltenham's present and future as chairman of the Racecourse Holdings Trust. It added up to an extra incentive, and no one was in any doubt that the best chance of a Henderson victory at this year's meeting would come in the first race on the Thursday card, the *Daily Express* Triumph Hurdle.

This is the championship race for juvenile (four-year-old) hurdlers, a colourful and often calamitous cavalry charge of up to thirty horses in which backers are invariably dumbfounded by a winner returned at the fanciful odds of 40 to 1 or more. Favourites do not have a great record in the race – indeed, since Peter O'Sullevan's Attivo won at 4 to 5 in 1974, the lowest-priced winner was Meladon at 6 to 1, and in both 1981 and 1982 the odds were 66 to 1.

This time, however, Henderson had every right to be confident. He not only saddled the favourite See You Then, recently bought into his stable after a brilliantly convincing win in Ireland, but also the second favourite Childown, who had won several of the major juvenile events in England and was now to be ridden by John Francome. But racing, and Cheltenham in particular, has a nasty habit of destroying dreams and, an hour before the race, Henderson was already being given reason to fret.

The cause of his initial problem was a query about the registration for See You Then. Right up to the deadline minute for declarations, there was an awful possibility that the horse would be withdrawn from the race through some trivial technicality. It was probably fortunate for the course security that the problem was resolved just in time as the wrath of the punters would have known no bounds; it was certainly fortunate for the increasingly desperate Henderson, an anxious, fidgeting man at the best of times and now showing every sign of worrying himself to breaking point.

If the public remained blissfully unaware of this backstage drama, they were equally oblivious of the embarrassment caused the previous lunch-time, when the ballot to reduce the Triumph field to the safety limit of thirty eliminated, among others, the horse owned by Lord Matthews, chairman of the sponsors Express Newspapers.

They might also not have noticed that, while the grateful Nicky Henderson emerged onto the parade ring and scurried from one to another of his fancied runners, his Lambourn neighbour Stan Mellor – who had trained the first and second in the race in 1983 – was supervising as much an experiment in animal behaviour as an attempt to complete a double. Son of a Gunner, the better of his two runners, was owned by Dr Desmond Morris, whose studies of human and animal life have made him a best-selling author. He was as interested in what went on before the race as during it.

The last hurdle in the 1984 Daily Express Triumph Hurdle which was won by Northern Game (far right) with See You Then (42) second and Manpower (33) third.

'It is,' said Dr Morris as he surveyed the paddock parade, 'all new to me. I feel as if we are in a roman amphitheatre.'

The atmosphere was now quite electric. The first day's crowd had topped 25,000, the second day – traditionally the quietest – had drawn 22,745, substantially up on the previous two years, and predictions for the Gold Cup crowd were anything above 40,000. Racecard sales profiled the surging interest in the Festival. First-day receipts for cards, selling at 50p a time, were £8,758 and the second day brought in £8,182. Together, this represented an increase of almost one hundred per cent on the receipts of two years earlier, when the racecards were, admittedly, 20p cheaper. The management were taking no chances for Gold Cup day and thirty thousand cards had been printed.

So this was the background to what should have been Nicky Henderson's day, a day for celebrations in Lambourn village and in the Hendersons' distinctive, brightly-painted house on the hill. But if the champagne was, metaphorically at least, on ice, that was where it stayed. Cheltenham can be generous in its giving of glory; it can also be savage in its disposal of disasters.

For Henderson, the day was ruined at the second hurdle. Just as the pack loomed in front of the stands for the first time, Francome felt the horse lose his action, feared the worst and pulled him up immediately. Childown, Nicky Henderson's personal favourite of all the horses in his yard, had broken a leg and was destroyed as swiftly and discreetly as is possible before forty thousand staring sets of eyes.

The race had to go on, and it seemed that Henderson would at least be taking sugar with his arsenic as Tommy Carmody brought See You Then with what looked a perfectly-timed run. He led over the last and onto the run-in, but the fates were determined that Henderson should have no reprieve from their malice. In the last few strides, See You Then was caught and overhauled by Edward O'Grady's Northern Game.

Has any trainer ever suffered so much heartache in one Festival race? You saddle the first two in the market, you try to convince yourself you don't really mind which of them wins ... and in the space of four viciously brief minutes, one hero is a fallen martyr, the other vanquished by next to nothing and forgotten in no time at all.

Someone would have to tell Peter French the result of the 'Triumph' – and every other race, come to that. There is no time to stand and stare for the acting chief of Racecourse Security Services. His eyes, and those of his nine inspectors dispersed around the betting areas of the course, are fixed on the public, not the horses.

RSS, the sport's private police force, do not come to Cheltenham to make themselves conspicuous or unpopular. Their aim is to be on hand to resolve disputes between punter and bookmaker, to patrol for possible forgery offences at the entrances and to be ready to assist the official resident police force in any way possible.

Their premises take the low profile to an exaggerated extreme. No one could accuse them of ideas above their station, based in a small stone hut behind the Tattersalls betting ring and near the hamburger stall. Unless one was in the know, the natural assumption would be that it was a shed for storing groundsman's equipment or number boards, rather than the 'nerve-centre' of an essential and highly-organised peacekeeping operation.

Over the course of the three days, the RSS men expected to deal with something over one hundred and fifty bookmaking disputes. Most of them would follow a familiar pattern – the punter returns with what he believes to be a winning ticket, only to be told by his bookie that he has the bet written down as being on a loser. In such a situation there is no easy way out because the truth is usually a slip of the tongue by the punter or a slip of the pen by the bookie's assistant, understandable in the general mêlée around every pitch which precedes each race at the meeting. There are doubtless instances when one or other party is deliberately trying to extort or withhold money, but short of accusing the person concerned of being a liar – which is not a course of action likely to produce the best results – there is a limit to the powers of the RSS inspectors. Usually, they seek to find a compromise which has the acceptance, albeit grudging, of both sides in the dispute. But even this is sometimes impossible. I followed one of the inspectors down into the ring with a racegoer who had taken the 'dispute procedure' and reported his claim to the men in the small stone hut in between races. He said he had placed a bet of £5 each way on a 12-1 shot which came in second and that the bookmaker had logged his bet on the wrong horse. Sure enough, politely and courteously as the RSS approach was made, the Brighton bookie involved grew more cantankerous with each new suggestion and the inspector finally had to close his notebook and retreat, regretfully explaining to the put-upon punter that, against such resentful opposition, there was nothing to be done. This, however, was a minority defeat; most of the RSS efforts to settle arguments are at least partially successful, and their role in stamping out badge offences over recent years has taken a great burden of worry away from racecourse officials and the regular police force.

There was no escape from the milling crowd, no quiet corner to lurk with a glass, a form guide and a few private thoughts. It was the kind of day on which one needed to decide instantly at the end of each race whether to have a drink, a bet or a pee. There was time for only one option and each one involved a long queue and a good deal of discomfort.

They say Gold Cup day has always been this way. Back in the not-so-distant days before plush new stands with carpeted floors, elevators and a Tote desk every few yards, the crush might have been still more claustrophobic, the day even more exhausting. Maybe not in 1926, when Tim Hamey won the Gold Cup, for it was then an event which still needed to prove itself. Certainly not in 1945, when old Davy Jones rode the winner, because home thoughts were still very much abroad, intent on weightier matters than even a steeplechasing classic. But in almost every year since, Prestbury Park has puffed under the strain of the sport's largest crowd, including Grand National Day. It is virtually impossible to test the capacity of a place like Cheltenham, where, if they felt inclined, countless thousands could gather in the centre of the course and still enjoy a reasonable view, but in 1984, what could be said with certainty was that there was not a spare seat, not an empty square foot of standing room in the Members' and Tattersalls areas. Many of the weak at heart and heavy of foot refuse to attempt Gold Cup day, unable to summon the mental reserves to cope with the crowd. But for many more, it is one of the year's magical days, when the hairs on the nape of the neck stand erect with anticipation in the minutes between the Foxhunters - that annual cavalcade of corinthian attitudes and colourful riding styles - and the parade for the classic chase of the year.

On the terrace up high behind the parade ring, the portly gentleman in the bowler hat was guarding an ever-shrinking collection of silverware. Nigel Dimmer could have passed for an undertaker, such is his deadpan expression and measured movements, but he is in fact the representative of Martin's the jewellers, for many years past the official suppliers of trophies to the Cheltenham course and the makers of the original 1823 Gold Cup. At Festival time, every cup, pot and shield, returned in hopefully good shape by the previous year's winner, is put on show for racegoers to ogle. A couple of tables in a miniature marquee take the strain, Mr Dimmer watches over them, answers the queries of the inquisitive and poses for dozens of pictures, then sees his treasures taken one by one down to the unsaddling enclosure for redistribution. The Foxhunters Trophy, the biggest of them all, had just gone for presentation to popular winner Oliver Sherwood and father Nat. The coveted and precious Gold Cup remained, awaiting its fate. Would it again go to one of Michael Dickinson's owners? Would one of Fred Winter's well-heeled owners carry it away? Or would Stan Riley's dream come true, with Jenny Pitman's Burrough Hill Lad capping a meteoric season with the greatest prize of all?

It had been an exacting few weeks for Mrs Pitman. What with being the emotional subject of *This is Your Life*, launching her autobiography with a party in the Cheltenham tented village and coping with a hundred and one pieces of mischievous conjecture about the health of her Gold Cup horse, she confessed herself in need of a good rest. She would not get it today.

Steadfastly, and with increasing tetchiness, Jenny had denied the rumours that Burrough Hill Lad was not 'right' and, as the parade for the race arrived and this splendidly made animal walked proudly onto the course, the suspicion that the muck had been spread by bookmakers anxious not to lay any further bets on the horse, grew to a probability. Burrough Hill Lad was unbeaten all season over fences; he had won his races with devastating ease and been so impressive that John Francome – who had been the fortunate jockey on each occasion – had said to the television audience: 'My only problem was in pulling the horse up. It will take a very good one to stop him winning the Gold Cup.'

But Francome was not on board now. He was claimed by Mr Winter to ride Brown Chamberlin and was now making properly confident noises about his chances on this one. Phil Tuck, his face still showing the scars of the badly broken nose which had painfully interrupted his season, resumed a partnership with 'The Lad' that he thought he had lost forever when Francome took over from him.

The heavy backers, however, appeared to believe there could be only one winner – the number one Dickinson challenger, Wayward Lad. True, he had recently been beaten by Brown Chamberlin, but there were excuses for that. He had won the valuable and prestigious King George VI Chase, the annual Christmas cracker at Kempton, for the second year running and now he was a worthy favourite to give Dickinson his third successive Gold Cup, all with different horses. Dickinson himself, tall and almost worryingly gaunt, his dark hair and well-toned sun-tan set off by a yellow freesia in his button-hole, would have had his usual early night and early morning – not for him the dares and derring-do of Festival nights on the town, not for him the remotest prospect of waking with a thick head. A bachelor, virtual teetotal and social shrinking violet, Dickinson could unkindly be accused of being a bore, and would probably not leap angrily to his own defence. 'I know people think I am narrow-minded,' he admits. 'But racing is everything to me. It is all that matters in my life.' Twelve months earlier, after achieving what had always seemed an impossibility by saddling the first five horses home in the Gold Cup, Dickinson had been asked how he could possibly follow the feat. 'By doing it again,' was his simple reply. But this year he had only two runners, and this year was to be his last Gold Cup – at least for the time being. Robert Sangster's cheque book had tempted him beyond the limits of loyalty to the jumping game and he would soon be set up in a lavish establishment to train on the flat. He intended to go out with a triumph.

Fred Winter would never train flat horses. He was past the age when he might have wanted to change course, but then I doubted if it had ever entered his head. He had borne the often callous setbacks of training jumpers, survived a heart scare and come to terms with himself to the point where he even took a mid-season holiday each year. He tinkered in his lovely Lambourn garden, played with his dogs and, to all who knew him, belied the initial gruff impression he can give with a warm friendliness which made him one of National Hunt's favourite people. If a Dickinson–Winter contest was settled on public popularity, Fred would win hands down. But it was to be settled on the course. They were locked in battle for the title of champion trainer, and now they were head to head in the biggest race of the year.

Even the chalets had mostly emptied for the main event. The Tote queues were enormous, the bars buzzed with anticipation and, out in the centre of the course, a latecomer hurried away from the helicopter shuttle service which had already ferried such distinguished guests as Clare Francis, Lord Vestey and Sheikh Ali Abu Khamsin to the track. The trainers, having given their charges a final encouraging slap on the neck and whispered their parting prayers, filed in anxious huddles from parade ring to stand. There was nothing more to be done.

Phil Hatcher came off the course, radio in hand, and stationed himself next to the wheelchair enclosure. Edward Gillespie and Philip Arkwright even managed to take a few minutes off from their endless duties to look in on the race which climaxed their year of planning. They were to see a spectacle which made their efforts seem wholly worthwhile, a race which made racing history of a very special kind, a race which made many punters rich and many bookies grind their teeth.

The Dickinson dream died first. As the field came past the stands for the second of three occasions on the 3¼-mile course which has been the Gold Cup distance since its inception, Bregawn – the 1983 winner – was clearly struggling or, perhaps more accurately in the light of his recent race behaviour, declining to perform. Wayward Lad showed briefly on the final circuit but by the top of the hill his challenge was over and the race belonged to Lambourn. It was Brown Chamberlin against Burrough Hill Lad, Fred Winter against the estranged wife of his former stable jockey, male against female, Francome fighting for his guv'nor against the horse he had ridden and tipped months earlier.

Brown Chamberlin had made virtually all the running, Francome waiting in front and gradually letting his horse accelerate. But at the second last, Burrough Hill Lad loomed up on his inner. Brown Chamberlin then jumped badly right at the last and, for all Francome's heroic straightening and steering, he was onto a loser. The big brown beauty, produced to perfection by Phil Tuck, stormed away up the hill to make Jenny Pitman the first woman ever to train a Gold Cup winner just as, less than a year earlier, she had been the first woman to train a National winner.

The ritual of the winner being welcomed back into the unsaddling area will never pale. Indeed, it has never been more emotional than now, with the new terracing allowing almost five thousand people to cheer the heroes in. Dozens more swept in behind the winning horse, even the extra security on the entrance to the enclosure powerless to keep them out. Edward Gillespie had joined the police and gatemen, but confessed: 'I stopped all the wrong people. In the general crush it was very hard to identify anyone at close quarters and among those I tried to keep out were Mrs Fred Winter and the Queen's Stud Manager.'

The press, when they could get close enough to speak to the connections in the throng of hangers-on and well-wishers, interviewed everyone in sight and, hardly surprisingly, Mrs Pitman took the opportunity to do some well-rehearsed 'I told you so' lines. Phil Tuck was rightly jubilant, but faintly worried. It turned out he was concerned about how he should address the Queen Mother when he was introduced. With this point of etiquette taken care of, he was led back into the changing-room, where, as ever, there were handshakes, backslapping and a crate of champagne to be devoured. Tuck, an under-rated northern-based rider, also signed his name on the wall next to his peg – a long-standing tradition for Gold Cup-winning jockeys. In his excitement he misspelt the name of his horse!

Jenny Pitman escaped from the hysteria and headed for the area in which her horse would undergo the compulsory dope-test. After the hubbub and emotion of the race and the subsequent reception, it was an incredibly quiet scene, and Jenny was determined to get a grip of her feelings and pretend it was just another day, just another winner. She took off her coat, straightened her dress and, making visible efforts to calm down, personally checked Burrough Hill Lad's legs. She was talking, either to herself or to the horse, for all she said was: 'We knew we could do it, didn't we?'

The Festival ended as it had begun. Michael Dickinson, who turned out Browne's Gazette to win Tuesday's opening race, a lifetime and more ago, finished his final Cheltenham with another winner, the odds-on Mighty Mac. It also ended as it had begun for Peter Scudamore and David Nicholson. The local pair were both still without a Festival winner between them despite more near misses than any man should have to tolerate. This time, Nicholson had three runners-up (although one was later relegated to fourth by a stewards' enquiry) and Scudamore was second past the post no fewer than five times. They teamed up in the final event of the meeting and the result was appropriate. Connaught River was second.

In the weighing-room later, Scudamore was suffering the inevitable ribbings for the jinx which appeared to afflict him every March, yet he was taking it all with a smile instead of a scowl, telling everyone who asked that he had enjoyed the three days more than any previous Cheltenham. 'Look at him,' said John Buckingham, the wise and experienced ex-jockey who once won the National on a 100 to 1 shot and now acts

In 1983 Jenny Pitman became the first lady to train a Grand National winner and she followed this up by training the 1984 Gold Cup winner, Burrough Hill Lad. Burrough Hill Lad is seen below returning in triumph with his jockey Phil Tuck.

as official valet and unofficial nursemaid and advisor to many a rider. 'He hasn't won a race and he's got every right to be depressed about it. But he's had a good time and he's come through with a smile on his face. That's what this game is all about – it's certainly what Cheltenham is all about.'

Outside, the Festival had not quite finished. There was life in the old day yet for all who wanted it, though some were plainly past their best. On the concourse behind the members' stand, a man stared doubtfully at a dustbin overflowing with empty bottles. Reaching a decision of some moment, he began to remove the bottles one by one, methodically breaking them by the neck and discarding them. Then, having created an almost flat surface, he gently sat on it and reached unsteadily for his wallet. His eyes opened in glazed bewilderment at the revelation that it was totally empty and he stared accusingly at it for some seconds before consigning it to the same fate as the broken bottles.

Racing may have finished, but there was still action on the course. A 'streaker', male and inebriated, was galloping up the home straight in his private impersonation of Burrough Hill Lad. He negotiated the final obstacle rather less gracefully than he would have liked, but recovered himself for a sprint to the line, cheered on wildly by a rapidly swelling crowd on the stand steps. No sooner was he past the post, however, than the police moved in to place helmets over his intimate parts in the now traditional treatment for such exhibitionists. It was more than three hours later that he was released and as he approached the coach party he had kept waiting, he began an impromptu song-and-dance routine, yelling 'I'm free' at the top of his still slurred voice.

It was the morning after, and nothing was quite the same. Faces which had been bright under pressure were now bleak with the return of normality. The course's Festival frills were disappearing and even the weather was greyer, colder and windier in sympathy.

Tim Spencer-Cox's troops were moving methodically through the debris and one outsized vacuum cleaner was in action on the rubbish-speckled members' lawn. The champagne bottles vanished into black plastic sacks and the flowers which had adorned every rooftop and every entrance were taken down and stacked outside Edward Gillespie's office like unwanted presents. The temporary stand was being dismantled, the caterers were starting their final clearing-up operation in the tented village and, on the course itself, Phil Hatcher and his men were beginning the backbreaking task of restoring the battered track to its former health. 'The night everyone goes home from the Gold Cup,' he explained, 'we start getting ready for the next one. This year it is not too bad, but the course can be a real mess after three days' racing in poor weather. I have seen it change from a lovely green to a ploughed field. We need a thousand tons of soil and eight or nine hundredweight of grass-seed to get it back to its best, and all of it is put down by hand, once we have located and replaced all the divots. It's farming at its best, but hard work.'

In the secretary's office, everyone was flat, approaching their menial tasks with a gloomy shortage of enthusiasm. As Rosemary Hammond explained: 'We are all on a high for three days. Getting back to the mundane duties comes very hard, no matter how many Festivals you have been through.'

Manager and clerk of the course were discussing the rights and wrongs of the meeting. General consensus was that it had been a good one. 'Things went wrong,' said Gillespie. 'They always will. No big meeting is perfect. People will criticise the security around the unsaddling enclosure and I am sure we will get complaints about the shortage of toilet facilities. It's true we just didn't have enough to cope but what we really need is to instal the longest urinal in the world – with no room for modesty!'

Philip Arkwright wore the look of a man who has had a weight lifted from his shoulders. Sitting under a hunting print and a nude calendar, his desk cluttered with papers and racecards, he agreed he was looking forward to going home at last. There was more racing to come at Cheltenham – a two-day meeting in April and the Hunters' evening programme in May, traditionally well-attended but 'one which is almost more difficult than the Festival meeting because so many of those involved only come here once a year and have no idea what to do'. But that was so far in the future, or so it seemed this morning, that it had no cause to trouble a man who had just come through the year's great challenge.

The financial returns from the Festival were staggering. Racing income, via the gate, racecards etc. amounted to around £1,250,000; the Tote reported a similar figure. But out of their proceeds, the course had substantial sums to pay, like £22,000 for police and £33,000 for staffing. There would, however, be plenty left.

Cheltenham has come a long way since that April day in 1902 when a horse called Both Ways won the Cowley Maiden Chase and launched the Cheltenham Festival's glittering career. It is now so important to the National Hunt world that, only hours after completing one year's Festival, owners, trainers and jockeys would already be contemplating the next.

Index